242

Day Brighteners

Day Brighteners

H. S. VIGEVENO

Vision House Publishers
Santa Ana, California 92705

New Testament Scripture quotations from the New Testament in Modern English, by J.B. Phillips, 1958, used by permission of the Macmillan Co.

Second Printing, September 1976

Copyright © 1976 by Vision House Publishing

Library of Congress Catalogue Number 76-12184
ISBN 0-88449-020-3

Printed in the United States of America.

CONTENTS

Part III—The Christian Life

PREFACE

For several years I have been writing one-minute radio spots. Often people have said, "Why don't you publish them?" I have always backed away because these spots were written with specific goals in view, such as reading the Bible, attending worship, or establishing a Christian home. And since they were written for radio, I didn't think they would hang together and make a book.

But it occurred to me that this approach could become a highly interesting and novel way of understanding a book in the Bible. So I applied myself to writing simple, short chapters on Paul's Letter to the Romans. This book is the result. It's original, since it was *not* written for radio.

Obviously *Day Brighteners* cannot be an exhaustive study of Romans, nor does it attempt to deal with some of the deeper issues raised by the text. But it serves as an introduction to the teaching of this crucial epistle. It will take you into the heart of Christianity, for Paul's Letter to Rome is really good news. The text used is the translation by J. B. Phillips, which I find to be the most exciting and helpful. You may read it as any other book or as a daily devotional guide. You will note a unique manner of paragraphing to make each reading crisp and clear.

1

GOOD NEWS FOR A BAD WORLD

If there's one thing that's pretty obvious,
it's this: there isn't much good news around.

You have to go looking for it.
You don't read it in the papers.
You don't hear it on the news.
You don't see it in our world.

Nobody seems to settle anything.

The conservatives keep fighting the liberals,
the capitalists fight the Communists,
and the right fight the left.

Races, nations, religions, and ideologies
remain in conflict.

Problems, nothing but problems everywhere.

Good news for our fast-paced society?

With all our nerves and tensions and anxieties?
Swallowing pills to pep up?
And more to calm down?

Having nervous breakdowns and crowding mental
institutions?

And always other people held in the grip of
alcohol, drugs, the almighty dollar,
or sexual deviations.

Good news for them?

Besides, we may blow ourselves to kingdom come
any day now.

Good news?
Who's kidding whom?

Maybe happiness is for kids.

Those were the days when you too believed in
Santa Claus and that good things happened around
Christmastime.

But that was a long time ago.
That dream's been shattered, but hard.

Does *the church* have any good news?

Church people are so outmoded, so often behind the
times,
so irrelevant.

Maybe those little old ladies believe that gospel.
They just sit there, smile, pray, and sing hymns.

But that's not good news for *you*!
You're not that old—yet.

Is there really any good news in our world?

Years ago one man said,

> *I am not ashamed of the gospel. I see it as
> the very power of God working for the
> salvation of everyone who believes it.*
> **—Romans 1:16**

14

He was a Christian.
He had become one against his will.

He was arrested by the living Christ on a trip he was taking
to silence some of Jesus' followers.

What happened to the Apostle Paul was good news
for him.

He believed it could become good news for
everybody.
He included the whole world!

And that means *you* are included, too.

2

WHAT IS THIS GOOD NEWS?

If you're not sick,
it's a cinch you won't call for a doctor.

Why should you?

But when you're feeling bad,
you'll give him a ring.

When everything's going great,
you're not looking for good news, either.

You're sitting on top of the world.

Good news is not for anyone
who's riding high, who's happy already.

So, good news isn't going to make any sense
unless things are pretty bad.

But that's the right time and place.
You need a doctor when you're sick.

Your need for God increases when you're desperate.

God reaches us in the depths of our miseries!

Not when we're sitting on top of the world.

Good news is only good for those who've got it bad.

That's when it begins to mean something:

> *I see in it God's plan for imparting
> righteousness to men, a process begun and*

> *continued by their faith. For, as Scripture says, "The righteous shall live by faith."*
> —**Romans 1:17**

And that's surely good news—
God making us whole.

How does it happen?

By faith.
Faith in what? In whom?

> *The gospel is centered in God's Son, a descendant of David by human genealogy and patently marked out as the Son of God by the power of that Spirit of holiness which raised Him to life again from the dead. He is our Lord, Jesus Christ.*
> —**Romans 1:3, 4**

God has done something for man.

He has personally visited this planet.
He has come for man's salvation.

And He will make the most desperate—righteous!

"God was in Christ personally reconciling the world to Himself—not counting their sins against them" (2 Corinthians 5:19).

And that is the *greatest* piece of news you'll ever hear!

PART I

THE HUMAN DILEMMA

"Bad as you please,
  you've felt they were
God's men and women still."
            —Robert Browning

3

MAN WITHOUT EXCUSE

A famous motion picture actor filed for bankruptcy.

He had made hundreds of movies
and millions of dollars.

But he owed half a million.
He blamed fast women and slow horses.

A plausible excuse but hardly a reason!

In the last analysis aren't *we* responsible
for our own failures?

Adam blamed Eve for taking the fruit.

Eve passed the buck to the serpent.

Excuses are easy to come by.

Only when you stop making excuses
will you see the light.

When you deceive yourself
even God can't do much for you.

Man must first see himself as he really is.
Not in his own eyes.
In God's eyes.

Not with his puny excuses,
but as he stands naked before his Creator.

Man knows very well that there is a God.
Still he pursues his own way.

He denies his Creator by his life and actions.
Therefore he's got himself in a pickle.

> *Since the beginning of the world the invisible attributes of God, e.g., His eternal power and deity, have been plainly discernible through things which He has made and which are commonly seen and known, thus leaving these men without a rag of excuse. They knew all the time there is a God, yet they refused to acknowledge Him as such.*
> —Romans 1:20, 21

That's why the good news only makes sense when we
stop excusing ourselves—
when we realize what we've done—
how we've turned our backs on God—
and why we're so sneaky about our sins.

But then, even for us, there's hope!

4

THE FOLLY OF MAN

Do you want to gain experience?
Why not?

What's wrong with a little experience?

You'll never know what anything is like
until you try it.

Grow up!
Find out for yourself what you've been missing!

How can you be free when you are confined
by so many restrictions?

How can you become mature as long as you remain
dependent?

Don't you think that *God* wants you to enjoy life?
Don't you think that He wants you to have some fun?

So, maybe you don't really understand God at all!
Maybe you have an immature concept of God,
onc which needs to be developed.

You are free to choose.

So, why not experience some thrills?
Live it up a little.

Everybody else does.

Why should *you* (of all people) deny yourself?
Don't you want to call the shots?

Once. Only once.
Why not be in charge, for once!

> *Behind a facade of "wisdom" they became just fools. . . . They gave up God, and therefore God gave them up—to be the playthings of their own foul desires.*
> **—Romans 1:22, 24**

And that is where our world has gone astray.

Man pushes the truth away from him,
but it remains the truth.

He wants someone to prove that God exists
while he closes his eyes to the evidence.

Evidence which screams at him everywhere.
Every day.

He thinks he is so clever
when, apart from God, he has become a fool.

He wants to run his own show.
He forgets that Someone else stages the performance.

Man can only see as far as his own nose.
And that isn't far enough.

5

MAN AND HIS LUSTS

The head coach of a professional football team
says that the worst thing about any player is . . .

If he is uncoachable!

That's a universal problem.
If man does not listen to the Coach,
he won't make it.

Man is out for kicks and tells you so.
He'll try anything.

He doesn't heed any warnings.
He has to get smashed up before he learns.

And sometimes he never learns!

He thinks he invents new ways of sinning,
when they're as old as Sodom and Gomorrah.

> *Women exchanged the normal practices of*
> *sexual intercourse for something which is*
> *abnormal and unnatural. Similarly, the*
> *men, turning from natural intercourse*
> *with women, were swept into lustful*
> *passions for one another. Men with men*
> *performed these shameful horrors,*
> *receiving, of course, in their own per-*
> *sonalities the consequences of sexual*
> *perversity.*
> **—Romans 1:26, 27**

The human mind is a delicate instrument.

Tamper with it

and you throw it out of balance.

That thing called "conscience" begins to act up.

It won't keep you from sinning,
but it may keep you from enjoying it.

(You'll try to quiet it down!)

But God has written certain eternal laws in our hearts.

We know right from wrong.
We cannot escape it.

And that's the point.

Why do we want to have our kicks?
Why do we want to be our own boss?
Why don't we listen to the warnings?

Because we like thrills and excitement?

No!

Because we like the thrill of breaking *God's* laws.
We are always in rebellion against *God*.

We want to be our own masters:

> **Since they considered themselves too high
> and mighty to acknowledge God, He
> allowed them to become the slaves of their
> degenerate minds.**
>
> **—Romans 1:28**

There you have the trouble with man.
That's why he needs the good news like all get-out.

He also needs a little coaching from the Head Coach.

6

MAN WITHOUT GOD

Down at Emergency Hospital in Los Angeles,
the place is really jumping on weekends.

That's when most of the victims of knifings,
stabbings, and shootings are brought in.

You wouldn't believe there was so much of it.

This Emergency Hospital keeps a staff of
a dozen doctors, nurses, and orderlies
running like crazy all night long.

And not just the rough stuff from the bars downtown.

Family and neighborhood brawls make their
contributions too.

"People are people.
You can't change them.
They're going to cut each other up.
They're going to fight."

That's the philosophy down at Emergency.

The bad guys get hauled into police stations too,
and put behind bars.

Our courts are filled with their cases.

But are those the *only* bad guys?

> ***They became whisperers-behind-doors,
> stabbers-in-the-back, God-haters; they
> overflowed with insolent pride and boast-***

fulness, and their minds teemed with diabolical invention. They scoffed at duty to parents, they mocked at learning, recognized no obligations of honor, lost all natural affection, and had no use for mercy.

—Romans 1:29-31

It doesn't really make much difference *what* you do.

Sin is rebellion.
All sin proceeds from the same core—the ego.

Man without God sets up his own rules.
He defies his Creator.

And whether he knifes somebody with a switchblade or with words doesn't make much difference.

All our sins are just different pieces cut from the same spoiled pie.

Besides, we reveal what we become.
Without God we encourage others to do what we do!

Being well aware of God's pronouncement that all who do these things deserve to die, they not only continued their own practices, but made no bones about giving their thorough approval to others who did the same.

—Romans 1:32

After all, how low can you get?

7

THE CRITIC

A lawyer had been watching a building
under construction across the street.

He turned to his associate and said,

"See that fellow over there?
I've been watching that loafer for the last two hours,
and he hasn't done a stroke of work."

But . . . how could the lawyer be doing much work
while he was watching out the window?

Whenever we play judge, we think we're beyond
reproach.

"Whatever I do, I like.
Whatever somebody else does, stinks."

When we criticize others,
we always fail to inspect ourselves.

While keeping our eyes on all those bad sinners,
we become blind to our own sins.

We pick at a splinter in someone else's eye,
while the log of lovelessness dangles from ours.

Generally, we are guilty of the things we criticize in
others.

They bother us so much
that we pay particular attention to them.

The person who is a liar is always on guard,
lest someone should lie to him.

The man of truth is not suspicious.

The thief is always expecting to be cheated.
The man of integrity is not worried.

The adulterer is leary of other people's morals.
But to the pure all things are pure.

If you think someone else has a nerve to brag,
you may be very conceited yourself.

If you don't think you are,
it's a sign that you're very proud indeed.

God sees the heart.
God is not as concerned with my actions
as He is with my self.

That's what really counts.

Our critical nature produces our own condemnation:

> *Now if you feel inclined to set yourself up
> as a judge of those who sin, let me assure
> you, whoever you are, that you are in no
> position to do so. For at whatever point
> you condemn others you automatically
> condemn yourself, since you, the judge,
> commit the same sins . . . . What makes
> you think that you, who so readily judge
> the sins of others, can consider yourself
> beyond the judgment of God?*
> **—Romans 2:1, 3**

Even the so-called good guys,
who manage to stay out of trouble with the law,
leave a lot to be desired!

8

ONLY ONE STEP

"Sorry to see you fellows leave,"
said the elevator operator to the ministers.
"You've been easy to get along with."

"You know," he added, "you deal with the public
and you get to know them."

He shook his head in disapproval.
We caught his inference.

We thought that we were easy to get along with too.
We were a pretty nice bunch of guys.

Why are we so eager to accept our goodness,
and why do we continually ignore the evil within?

We play up our attributes
and forget our liabilities.

As long as we see ourselves in that light,
we look rather good.

And as long as we keep comparing ourselves with
others,
we make sure we come out on top!

It feeds our ego.

But there is another way to view ourselves.

What would happen if we compared ourselves
with a perfect standard?

We are not what we ought to be.

Or want to be.
Or would be.

What would happen if, even for a moment,
we compared ourselves with Jesus?

With man as he ought to be?

With the true man, the ideal man?

As long as we see ourselves in our own light,
we look pretty good.

As soon as we enter His presence,
it's a different story.

Then we realize that we have to take a step.
Only one step will do.

> *Don't you realize that God's kindness is
> meant to lead you to repentance? Or are
> you by your obstinate refusal to repent
> simply storing up for yourself an ex-
> perience of the wrath of God?*
> **—Romans 2:4**

The step of repentance means a change of direction.
It's the only step that will get you moving forward.

9

JUSTICE FOR ALL

The leader of an uncivilized tribe put it this way:

"If I take someone else's wife, that's good.
If someone else takes my wife, that's bad."

Every man has a sense of right and wrong.
Conscience is universal.

All human beings believe that they should behave according to certain standards.

But the fact is that they do not behave that way.

They know the law
but they break it.

Surely this is the most obvious fact about man.

Can our acceptance of law save us?
Or our familiarity with what God demands?

Can our conscience keep us
from the inevitable punishment of evil?

Something else is needed.

Obedience.
Truth.

> *All who have sinned without knowledge of the Law will die without reference to the Law, and all who have sinned knowing the Law shall be judged according to the Law. It is not familiarity with the Law that*

justifies a man in the sight of God, but obedience to it .... For there is no preferential treatment with God.
—Romans 2:12, 13, 11

Just are the ways of God.
Just will be the judgment.

Man is unjust, but God is just.

We rightly fear to fall into the hands of a just God.
We can only rejoice that He is merciful, too.

All men will be treated aright by Him.

The religious and the heathen.
Regardless of race or nationality.
Regardless of status or geographical location.

And this is our hope:

"Mercy smiles in the face of judgment" (James 2:13).

10

SECRETS

A Broadway star was boasting about her psychiatrist.

"He's the greatest," she said.
"You can't imagine what he's done for me.
Everybody ought to try him."

"But I don't need analysis," said a friend,
"I couldn't be more normal.
There's nothing wrong with me."

"Oh," she replied, "he's absolutely great.
He'll find *something* wrong!"

Is that your opinion of man?

Pretty normal, after all.
It takes a psychiatrist to find something wrong?

We generally consider man to be rather good.
We all try to live by the golden rule.

Some people may turn bad,
but even so they're still basically O.K.

Is this realistic enough?

What are we like within?

Is there no defection, no rebellion,
no selfishness in our innermost selves?

What of our dreams, our imaginations, our motives?
What about our secret sins?

Would we want the doors opened on all our dirty closets?

Are we willing to have a complete inspection of *everything*?

> **In the Day of True Judgment . . . God will judge men's secret lives by Jesus Christ.**
> **—Romans 2:16**

Man without God, without hope,
under the scrutiny of God
hasn't a chance.

Something else is needed.

And that something else has been done.
Someone has taken his place in death.

Even from the fearful aspects of judgment.
That's the top of the news in Jesus Christ.

11

EVEN FOR YOU!

You're not one of those bad guys.
You're not one of those critical good guys either.

You're a Christian.
You believe in God.

You read your Bible.
You pray.
You tithe.
You go to church.

It's never crossed your mind that you're not saved.

You don't depend on your good works to get you to
heaven.
You believe.
You do God's will.

You know what He wants of you.
And everything is right between you and God.

You're so sure of the way to God that
you could point it out to a blind man.

But have you ever asked yourself why
Jesus told God's chosen people that, with all their
religion,
they were *not* saved?

(It never crossed their minds that they were not!)

They were God's representatives.
They knew God.
They obeyed His law.
They did His will.

They tithed and prayed and read their Bibles.

In spite of all their religious activity,
they failed to recognize Jesus as the Son of God.

It was religious people who rejected Him.
The high priest called the Son of God a blasphemer.

Believers in God crucified Him!
And they believed they were doing the will of God!

What had gone wrong?

Sometimes religion makes people conceited,
egotistical,
secure, and blind.

Know-it-alls become proud of their faith.
Nobody can tell them anything.

They are safe and secure in their traditions.
A false security produces self-righteous prigs.

And in their pride they slam the door on God.

> *You have a certain grasp of the basis of
> true knowledge. You have without doubt
> very great advantages. But, prepared as
> you are to instruct others, do you ever
> teach yourself anything? You preach
> against stealing, for example, but are you
> sure of your own honesty? You denounce
> the practice of adultery, but are you sure
> of your own purity?*
> **—Romans 2:20-22**

Real Christianity makes you examine your inner self.
Real Christianity means you'd better look within!

12

PHONY CHRISTIANS

When a Muslim gets drunk they say,
"He has left Muhammad and gone over to Jesus."

What an indictment that is!

Surely this is not due to the witness
of our Christian missionaries, is it?

Isn't it the result of our Western businessmen,
who are products of our Christian heritage?

Why do so many people stay away from church?
Why do so many accuse Christians of hypocrisy?
Why do they call Christians phonies?

Is this why they reject Jesus Christ?

There are relatively few converts to Christ
because of the way most of us live.

Are we dependable, honest, kind, trustworthy,
compassionate, loving, truthful, concerned?

It's all so obvious to everyone else.
They see through our religious paraphernalia.

And they don't like what they see.
That's why they don't become Christians.

The world thinks that God has failed
in making Christians no better than they are.

He must be some God . . . !

Let's be honest.
It isn't all *their* fault that they reject Christ.

Of course the Devil has blinded them.
They fail to see the truth.

But you can't put all the blame on the Devil.
We have to accept a large share ourselves.

There is hypocrisy among Christians.

And there is also pride, jealousy, gossip,
criticism, negativism, prejudice, and intolerance.

> **Everyone knows how proud you are of the Law, but that means a proportionate dishonor to God when men know that you break it! Don't you know that the very name of God is cursed among the Gentiles because of the behavior of Jews?**
> **—Romans 2:23, 24**

What Paul says here of the religious Jew
must surely be applied to Christians as well.

13

REAL CHRISTIANS

A woman was sitting in her parked car
watching a police officer checking parking meters.

He stopped at the car in front of her,
took out a dime, and dropped it into the meter.

She was amazed and went to him.
She said,

"That was one of the nicest things
I've seen in a long time."

"Well, don't get all choked up, lady," he replied;
"That happens to be my wife's car."

What really means much to us?

The good deed.
The out-of-the-way kindness.
Actions from the heart.

That overshadows religious affirmations.
That's more important than our creeds.

Isn't even a cup of cold water given in Jesus' name
an eloquent sermon?

But what makes a person behave like this?
How do evil men change their actions?

Before you can produce good fruit,
you must have a healthy tree.

With a good tree you get results.

So the tree is more important than the fruit.

A diseased tree cannot bring forth good fruit. A good tree cannot produce bad fruit.

Man's relationship to God is always first.

If that is genuine, the good life will follow. It's the heart that matters.

> *The true Jew (Christian) is one who belongs to God in heart, a man whose circumcision is not just an outward physical affair but is a God-made sign upon the heart and soul, and results in a life lived not for the approval of man, but for the approval of God.*
>
> **—Romans 2:29**

After all, we will not be judged by what we believe, but by what we have done in the obedience of faith.

Not according to our faith, but according to our works.

14

THE STRAIGHT EDGE OF THE LAW

Two men were arrested for possession
of a pair of loaded dice.

In court each accused the other of owning them.

Unable to get to the truth,
the judge asked the arresting officer,

"Officer, did you take these dice without a search
warrant?"

"Yes, your honor."

"You had no right to," continued the judge;
"Give them back immediately."

One of the two stuck out his hand,
and the judge promptly sentenced him to thirty days!

When the final test comes,
no one will escape,
since no one has lived up to every detail of the Law.

> *No man can justify himself before God by
> a perfect performance of the Law's
> demands — indeed it is the straight-edge
> of the Law that shows us how crooked we
> are.*
> **—Romans 3:19, 20**

That is clear *now*.
Who can stand before the obligatory, all-demanding,
perfect Law of God?

There is none righteous, no, not one. There is none that understandeth, there is none that seeketh after God; they have all turned aside, they are together become unprofitable; there is none that doeth good, no, not so much as one. . . . Destruction and misery are in their ways, and the way of peace have they not known; there is no fear of God before their eyes.
—Romans 3:10-12, 16-18

Man has alienated himself from God.
By choice.

That defection is universal.
And that is the mystery. . . .

Man remains evil,
though he sometimes tries to be good.

Man keeps hiding from God,
though at times he also goes looking for Him.

15

WHAT'S YOUR BATTING AVERAGE?

There are all kinds of ball players.

There's the poor player who bats .180.
There's the good player who gets .275.
And there's the champ who comes up with .364.

No one manages a perfect average for the season
and hits every time he's up there swinging.

Man falls short of perfection.

He fouls out or strikes out again and again.
All in all it's a pretty poor performance.

You can't count on a hit every time.
Even for the best of men.

This, then, is our dilemma.

We fall short of the ideal.
We miss the mark.

The bad guys don't measure up.
The good guys think they do but they don't.

And the religious who try hard are a disappointment,
if not to others, at least to themselves.

> *I have shown above that all men from
> Jews to Greeks are under the condem-
> nation of sin. . . . There is no distinction
> to be made anywhere: everyone has
> sinned, everyone has fallen short of the
> beauty of God's plan.*
> **—Romans 3:9, 23**

45

Day Brighteners from Romans

Man is hopeless.
He can only hope in Christ.

He stands condemned but he can find a way out.

That spells out good news for everyone.
No one ever needs to feel excluded.

Good news: God loves rebellious man.

The good news is that God accepts man in revolt.
The good news is focused in Jesus Christ.

It's the best news you'll ever hear.

Jesus came to seek and to save the lost.
The whole world.
And that includes you.

Even with your batting average!

PART II

THE DIVINE SOLUTION

"When Christ came into my life,
I came about like a well-handled ship."
—Robert Louis Stevenson

16

BEGINNING ALL OVER AGAIN

Have you ever dreamed of beginning again?
Of having a clean slate?

Of starting all over anew?
Like you feel at the beginning of a new year?
Only more so?

Wouldn't it be great to believe that's possible?
Even for all of us rebels?

But it wouldn't be good news
if you didn't have a chance.

If you were stuck in the same old rut
and couldn't get out.

What would be exciting about that?

"You can't change human nature!"

We *can* begin again.
Jesus tells us so.

We *can* have a clean slate.
It's a new birth.

All that you are you need not remain.
All that you want to be you can become.

Since we all come under condemnation
for failing to meet the requirements
of the law of God,
there must be an answer.

God provides that answer.

He enters personally into the world.
He lives in our midst.
He suffers the consequences of sin.

He freely takes our judgment on himself at the Cross.
He is punished in our place.

Jesus did not have to die.
"It was the suffering that He bore that has healed
you" (1 Peter 2:24).

God offers us a new start.
And a new life.

> *Under this divine "system" a man who has
> faith is now freely acquitted in the eyes of
> God by His generous dealing in the
> redemptive act of Jesus Christ.*
> **—Romans 3:24**

So what more could you ask for?

All that you are you need not remain.
All that you want to be you can by His grace become!

17

THE GREAT POSSIBILITY

Everything Jesus touched, He changed.

He touched the lame, and they could walk.
He touched the blind, and they could see.
He touched the lepers, and they were made whole.

He touched greedy, selfish Zaccheus,
and that little man became benevolent and selfless.

He touched the life of a woman in adultery.
Freed of her guilt, she started on a new road.

He touched the cross—man's invention
of inhuman punishment and torturous death.
Now it is the symbol of faith and salvation.

He removed the fear of death.
He arose triumphantly from the tomb.

Jesus touched the uncivilized tribes of Europe
and became responsible for Western culture
with its compassion for the sick, the downtrodden,
and the helpless.

He influenced our music and art,
drama and literature, philosophy and government.

Everything Jesus touched, He changed.

He can also change you.
That is the great possibility.

Jesus did not come to enable *us* to save *ourselves*.

Nor did He die to *help* us save ourselves.
He came to *save* us.

Look at the Cross.
It's central.

What happened there makes it possible
to begin all over again.

> *God has done this to demonstrate His righteousness both by wiping out the sins of the past (the time when He withheld His hand) and by showing in the present time that He is a just God and that He justifies every man who has faith in Jesus Christ.*
>
> **—Romans 3:25, 26**

Yes, *every* man!

18

BELIEVING INSTEAD OF ACHIEVING

Air can fill any vacuum.
There is plenty of it.

Even if all the people in the world
would breathe in at the same time,
we couldn't use it all up.

The grace of God is like air:
Abundant, free, plentiful.

A large sign attracts you when you drive into
the town of Trenton, New Jersey:

TRENTON MAKES — THE WORLD TAKES.

God makes Himself available to man.
It's as simple as that.
We need but receive His love.

Is that too easy?
Is that damaging to our pride?
Believing instead of achieving?

Is that cheap?
Like air?
Free to everyone?

Is there no cost involved?

A price *was* paid,
a costly price—a life was forfeited.

A noble, selfless life,

the life of the Son of God.

Jesus suffered in our place.

He took our punishment.
He accepted what we deserved.

If we can only see the Cross like that,
we will never again consider the grace of God cheap!

No one merits the love of God.

Not the good or the bad.
Not the rich or the poor.
Not the educated or the uneducated.
Not the white or the black.
Not the Christian or the atheist.

> *What happens now to human pride of achievement? There is no more room for it. Why, because failure to keep the Law has killed it? Not at all, but because the whole matter is now on a different plane—believing instead of achieving.*
> **—Romans 3:27**

But that, in itself, spells good news for all!

19

JUSTIFIED!

Suppose you are arrested
under suspicion of committing a crime
and are hauled into court.

You declare your innocence.
Your lawyer proves that you were not guilty.

The judge allows you to leave the court
without a stain on your character.

Since you are innocent, you are completely justified.

But what if you are guilty?

The judge may rebuke you.
But since it is a first offense,
you may leave the court without any penalty
inflicted.

You are free.
Although not cleared of the charge, you are forgiven.

Among men the guilty can be *forgiven,*
but only the innocent can be *justified.*

Yet God not only forgives the guilty.
He *justifies* them.
He removes all the charges.
He restores us to the divine favor.

He pronounces us righteous before Him.
He treats us, because of His exhaustless love,
as if we were actually *good!*

Not all our sins can cancel out His love.
He looks upon us as though we had not sinned.

Not that our rebellion did not matter.
We are totally guilty.

Our rebellion required a cross.
Our revolt was against God Himself.

But justification means that we are
actually pronounced innocent!

In spite of all our actual guilt.
"Just as if we had not sinned."

> *We see now that a man is justified before*
> *God by the fact of his faith in God's*
> *appointed Saviour and not by what he has*
> *managed to achieve under the Law.*
> **—Romans 3:28**

It may be hard to believe.
But it's actually going to be harder not to.

20

THE GIFT OF GOD

A mother once went to Napoleon
to ask pardon for her son.

He was guilty of his second serious military offense.

"I do not seek justice," she said;
"I plead for mercy."

"Why?" replied Napoleon. "He does not deserve
mercy."

"It would not be mercy if he deserved it, Sire!
Mercy is all I ask for."

The Emperor had mercy and spared her son.
Not that he deserved it.

The gift of mercy does not come upon the deserving.

If we work for something, we expect pay.
If we have earned wages, they should rightfully be
given us.

But a gift cannot be worked for.
A gift is entirely free.

> *Now if a man works, his wages are not
> counted as a gift but as a fair reward. But
> if a man, irrespective of his work, has faith
> in Him who justifies the sinful, then that
> man's faith is counted as righteousness,
> and that is the gift of God.*
> **—Romans 4:4, 5**

You can only accept a gift.
You can receive it and be thankful.
And you can express your thanks.

This gift is received by faith.

"Faith is a living, daring confidence in God's grace, so sure and certain that a man would stake his life on it a thousand times," said Martin Luther.

Such faith believes the God who justifies the undeserving.

That's why it is not a vain hope.

21

SENSE AND NONSENSE

"See that building there? That's the library,"
Lucy tells Charlie Brown.
"If you ever want to borrow a book,
all you have to do is go in there
and tell them which one you want,
and they'll let you take it home."

"Free?" asks Charlie.
"Absolutely free," she replies.

And Charlie muses:
"Sort of makes you wonder what they're up to!"

Do you wonder what *God* is up to?

He offers free forgiveness.
His mercy is a gift.

What's the catch?
No catch!

Either this is the road we walk,
or else we have to create our own way.

With good deeds,
by keeping the law,
and working for our salvation.

But can we ever become good enough?

It's either/or, not both/and.

It's either by promise or by law.

Either by faith or by works.
Either a gift or you pay for it.
Either believing or achieving.

> *If, after all, they who pin their faith to keeping the Law were to inherit God's world, it would make nonsense of faith in God Himself, and destroy the whole point of the Promise.*
>
> **—Romans 4:14**

So if you believe in the grace of God
how can you also pin your faith to the Law?

The one is exclusive of the other.

The Law leads to uncertain death.
Grace offers the promise of a new life.

Which would you rather choose?

It makes good sense:

> *The whole thing, then, is a matter of faith on man's part and generosity on God's.*
>
> **—Romans 4:16**

22

LIVING BY FAITH

A professor at Yale University said,

"I never consciously gave up a religious belief.
I just put my beliefs into a drawer.
When I opened it there was nothing there at all."

Faith is not sitting back and doing nothing.
What you believe can't be stuck in drawers.

Then it will get as outmoded as the Model A Ford.

The faith you have is the faith you show.

It is neither fantasy nor sentiment.

It's for the road.
It's where the action is.
It's life.

Consider that great man of faith, Abraham.

He put his confidence in God, utterly.
And that made all the difference for him.

He stepped out on faith.
He left his country and his people.

He went in search of a country God had promised.
He didn't know where to go.
But he started traveling anyway.

He believed prior to any signs.

The sign of circumcision (which has remained

as a symbol of God's covenant with His people)
was given him as a seal of faith.

Abraham did not believe because of the sign.
He believed first, and then God gave the sign.

He was promised to become a father of many nations.
But he had no son.

And he was practically a hundred years old
when he believed that!

> *With undaunted faith he looked at the
> facts. . . . Yet he refused to allow any dis-
> trust of a definite pronouncement of God
> to make him waver.*
> **—Romans 4:19, 20**

This was the dynamic by which Abraham lived,
the ongoing reality of faith.

He was absolutely convinced of God's
trustworthiness.
It really made all the difference.

> *He drew strength from his faith, and,
> while giving the glory to God, remained
> absolutely convinced that God was able to
> implement His own promise. This was the
> "faith" which was "counted unto him for
> righteousness."*
> **—Romans 4:21, 22**

Isn't that much better than
putting your faith in a drawer?

23

PEACE!

Most people want peace of mind.
They go for it like a touchdown in football.

"That's what I need," they say.
"I've got to have peace."

But that's hardly the way to find it.

Can you *make* yourself peaceful?
Can you work yourself up into peace?

Isn't it rather something that must happen to you?
Isn't it rather like happiness, a by-product?

Aren't there certain conditions to be met?

> "We would have inward peace,
> Yet will not look within;
>
> We would have misery cease,
> Yet will not cease from sin;
>
> We want all pleasant ends,
> But will use no harsh means."
> —Matthew Arnold

Peace is the result of the good news.
The good news tells you that you can have peace.

Through repentance.
And faith.
And self-honesty.

Not only be at peace with yourself, but with God.

This peace becomes a reality when you know you are *accepted*.

It only comes when you know you are forgiven.

Forgiveness is the free offer of Jesus Christ.
His death on the Cross justifies you.

You are no longer considered guilty.
You are pronounced righteous in His eyes.

This you can receive freely.
It is the gift of God.

> *Since then it is by faith that we are justified, let us grasp the fact that we have peace with God through our Lord Jesus Christ.*
> **—Romans 5:1**

Everyone desires peace.
Few will meet the conditions, the simple conditions, that produce inner heartfelt peace.

That is the experience of the repenter.
That is the happiness of the justified.

24

HERE I STAND

Have you ever attempted to see a celebrity?

It wasn't easy, was it?
They are usually well-protected.

You cannot get past the agent to see the actor.

You get stopped by secretaries when you
seek out the head of a corporation.

And what a rigmarole it would be
to get to the President of the United States!

There are, of course, those who manage it.
They know how.

Perhaps they are even related to the celebrity.

Some government dignitaries experience difficulty
in seeing the President,
but not the President's children.

Why not?
Because of their relationship.

What happens to us when we become Christians?

We are accepted into the family of God.
We enter a new relationship.

We are received because of Jesus Christ.
The Son of God calls us his brothers and sisters.

Through Him we have confidently entered into this new relationship of grace, and here we take our stand, in happy certainty of the glorious things He has for us in the future.

—Romans 5:2

Here we stand.
In certainty and faith.

It's actually true.
There need be no doubt about it.

This is the good news.

The Creator of the universe loves us.
He has sent His only Son to die for us.

The Son sets us free from the bondage of sin.
We are taken into the family of God.

Not only do you accept Christ.
He also accepts you!

25

HERE AND NOW

The white Queen tells Alice (in *Through the Looking Glass*):

"The rule is jam tomorrow and jam yesterday, but never jam today."

Why not?

Can we live happily in yesterday?
Or can we be content always looking to the future?

A girl in an office wears a locket: "Jam Today."
Why not?

The Devil would like the whole human race "hag-ridden by the future."

Constantly in pursuit of the rainbow's end.

"Never honest, nor kind, nor happy *now*," writes C. S. Lewis.

The Christian cannot live just for the hereafter. He lives in the here and now.

Joyously.
Hopefully.
In spite of all his trials.

How can you learn anything in life apart from trouble?

How can you gain patience without battling impatience?

How can you grow in faith unless you cope with
doubt?
How can you gain humility unless you fight pride?
How can you be loving unless you combat hatred?

Is it not precisely through those battles
that you learn the most?

Don't you find yourself maturing in suffering?

Isn't it true that this is how you draw nearer to God?

Not during calm seas but in the storm?

Our experience of God deepens in the depths.

The Cross is the place of encounter.
The Cross draws God into the heart of suffering.

And that is the point of our hope *now*.

> *This doesn't mean, of course, that we have
> only a hope of future joys — we can be full
> of joy here and now even in our trials and
> troubles. Taken in the right spirit these
> very things will give us patient endurance;
> this in turn will develop a mature
> character, and a character of this sort
> produces a steady hope, a hope that will
> never disappoint us.*
> **—Romans 5:3-5**

Jam today!

26

LOVE SO AMAZING

A motion picture actress made it to the top.
She was greatly in demand.

"I'm going along the crest now," she said
in an exclusive interview.

"I'm enjoying the ride.
I've got everything I want,
and I don't think everything's happening too fast.
Hell, no, I think I deserve it."

Perhaps so, in man's world.
But not in God's world.

Man does not deserve anything.

Man in revolt, rebelling against his Creator,
deserves only judgment.
And he's on his way there.

He is not worthy of the love of God.
He is not worthy of the death of Christ.

Some may think God owes them salvation.

But those who know how far short
they have fallen of God's standard
are ready to believe differently.

Christ died for sinners.

Not for the best.
Not for the good.
Not for the worthy.

Not for the deserving.

But *only* for the undeserving.

> *In human experience it is a rare thing for one man to give his life for another, even if the latter be a good man, though there have been a few who have had the courage to do it. Yet the proof of God's amazing love is this: that it was while we were sinners that Christ died for us.*
> —Romans 5:7, 8

Look at the Cross!
It gives the divine perspective!

If you cannot see the love of God *there*,
you will probably see it nowhere else.

> "When I survey the wondrous cross
> On which the Prince of Glory died,
> My richest gain I count but loss,
> And pour contempt on all my pride."
> —Issac Watts

27

LOVE CASTS OUT FEAR

"Shut your eyes to things you are afraid of.
Pretend they don't exist.
Put them out of your mind."

That's not good enough.
You'll need more than that to battle your fears.

Two people were talking about their horoscopes.

"I didn't know you believe in astrology," said one.
"Oh," replied the other, "I believe in everything —
a little bit."

That's not good enough cither.
You'll need more faith than that to battle life's fears!

"I'm scared of that big lion of yours," said he,
trying to humor the little boy with his balloon.

"Don't be scared," said the boy;
"you ought to see how small he looks
when I let out the air!"

God alone can remove our blown-up fears.

Fears in the present.
Fears of the past.
Fears of the future.
Fears of judgment.

If we believe that God sent His Son for us,
is it not reasonable to believe He loves us?

If we believe that Christ gave His life for us,
is it not reasonable to accept that love confidently?

And if He triumphed over death,
why should we fear the unknown?

Security is the result of the gospel.
God's demonstrated love removes our fears.

It's hardly enough to believe in everything a little bit.
It is possible to rest completely in the grace of God.

Know you are forgiven.
Know you are accepted.
Consider yourself justified.
The guilt is removed.

And with it, all your bogus fears.

> *Moreover, if He did that for us while we
> were sinners, now that we are men
> justified by the shedding of His blood,
> what reason have we to fear the wrath of
> God? If, while we were His enemies,
> Christ reconciled us to God by dying for
> us, surely now that we are reconciled we
> may be perfectly certain of our salvation
> through His living in us.*
> **—Romans 5:9, 10**

How could it be good news,
if it cannot remove our fears?

28

MAN #1 AND MAN #2

"Adam sat on a garden wall.
Adam rebelled and had a great fall.
And all our researchers
And government men
Cannot put the children of Adam
Together again."

Adam came from the hand of God.
But Adam desired independence.

Adam believed in himself more than in God.
He wanted his freedom.

Through Man #1 sin entered the world.
And with sin came death and judgment.

Man #1 was responsible for it all.
But we are responsible too.

We desire our freedom from God.
We also believe in ourselves.

We yield to temptation.
and are guilty of insurrection.

Then Man #2 came from the hand of God.
Man #2 was the Son of God.

He was placed in the midst of temptation.
He did not surrender.

He resisted the Devil.
He triumphed over sin and death.

He won the victory.

Through Man #1 sin entered the human race.
Through Man #2 grace is available to all.

All who follow in the steps of Man #1 will die.
All who follow in the steps of Man #2 will live.

All who continue the ways of Man #1 will be condemned.
All who yield to the power of Man #2 are justified.

All the followers of Man #1 will face the judgment.
All the relatives of Man #2 will enter the Kingdom.

> *If one man's offence meant that men should be slaves to death all their lives, it is a far greater thing that through Another Man, Jesus Christ, men by their acceptance of His more-than-sufficient grace and righteousness should live all their lives like kings! ... One man's disobedience placed all men under the threat of condemnation, but One Man's obedience has the power to present all men righteous before God.*
> **—Romans 5:17, 19**

Are you with Man #1 or Man #2?

29

THE SIMPLE TRUTH

There is something that is true for all men.
Therefore it is also true for you.

There is something that is always true.
Therefore it is true now.

There is something that was true before you were
born.
Therefore it is true after you believe.

It is a simple fact.
It is the good news.

God loves all men in the world.
You are just one person in that world.
Like every other person.
No difference.

Therefore you too are loved by God.

Nothing can prevent God from loving you.
Nothing can keep Him from accepting you.

All people are bad, including you.
But Jesus has already died for you.

It was finished on that Cross.

That is the great *fact*.

He knows your sins better than you do.
He is aware of all that goes on within you.

Strange and wonderful as it may seem, He still loves you.
That does not keep Him from accepting you!

It would not be grace if we earned it.

It's not an afterthought when the Law failed.
It's not a consolation prize after you lost.

No, it's the first thing.
Before everything else.

It was there from the beginning—
in the garden of Eden.

It will be there at the end—
in the Kingdom of God.

The rest of our theological luggage can wait.
This is the first piece.

God is the God of all grace.

> *Though sin is shown to be wide and deep, thank God His grace is wider and deeper still! The whole outlook changes .... Grace is the ruling factor, with righteousness as its purpose and its end the bringing of men to the eternal life of God through Jesus Christ our Lord.*
> **—Romans 5:20, 21**

His love is for all and therefore for me.

His love is for me and therefore for all.

PART III

THE CHRISTIAN LIFE

"Christianity is a battle,
   not a dream."
            —Wendell Phillips

30

EXPLOITATION

An old-time evangelist named Gypsy Smith
tells this humorous story;

"I say, Jack," said a friend, "I hear you got
converted."

"Yes, I have. Praise God!" said Jack.
"I've even joined the church."

"Well, d'you remember some time ago
I lent you some money?"

"Yes, uh—I remember."

"I'll expect you to pay it back.
When people get religious,
we expect them to do what's right."

"Oh," said Jack, "the Lord has pardoned all my
sins—
and that's one of them."

A Christian who doesn't pay his debts
isn't much of a Christian!

It doesn't take much to see
that such a Christian is exploiting his salvation.

A Christian who follows the temptations of the Devil
is not living as a member of his new family.

Not that we can reach perfection.
We cannot accomplish the impossible.

Even for the best of us, life is difficult.
The Christian is never free from struggle.

The battle continues between flesh and spirit.
It's a fierce fight—a real conflict.

> "When the fight begins within himself,
> A man's worth something.
> God stoops o'er his head,
> Satan looks up between his feet.
> Both tug—he's left, himself, in the middle.
> The soul wakes and grows.
> Prolong that battle through his life.
> Never leave growing till the life to come."
>   —Browning

Who dares to take advantage of the generosity of God?

> *Shall we sin to our heart's content and see how far we can exploit the grace of God? What a ghastly thought! We, who have died to sin—how could we live in sin a moment longer?*
>   **—Romans 6:1, 2**

Something should have happened to a Christian.
God's love sets him in a new direction.

If he exploits the goodness of God,
he isn't much of a Christian.

In fact, he's probably not one at all.

31

BREAKING THE POWER OF SIN

What's your biggest problem?

Other people?
Money?
Sex?

Evil thoughts?
Patience?
Nerves?
Anxiety?

Accepting the past?
Coping with the present?
Fear of the future?
If you could only solve that one problem,
you'd feel like a new person.

Do you compare yourself with a surfer,
dragging out his board against the angry waves,
struggling to get beyond the breakers?

Wouldn't you rather come riding in,
standing like a conquering hero on that board,
with the power of the ocean behind you?

Why not?
Whom do you believe?

What does it mean that God is *God*?

Even though you cannot trust yourself,
what does it mean to trust *Him*?

Jesus did not cater to sin.
He overcame the flesh.

He defeated the Devil.
He rose from the dead.

Here, then, is the secret of the Christian life:
Identify with Jesus Christ.

He died—we died with him.
He rose—we rose with him.

We share in his death and resurrection.
Therefore our old selves lose their hold on us.
A new pattern of living replaces the old.

This is the fact!
Recognize it.
Believe it.

> *We can be sure that the risen Christ never dies again—death's power to touch Him is finished. He died because of sin once; He lives for God forever. In the same way look upon yourselves as dead to the appeal and power of sin but alive and sensitive to the call of God through Jesus Christ our Lord.*
>
> **—Romans 6:9-11**

That's the good news!

New life is possible.
By the grace of God.

Like a surfer, running risks, living dangerously,
but with the power of the living God behind you!

32

THE POWER OF THE WILL

When you think of power, what do you think of?

The latest, fastest car with the most powerful engine?
The jet streaking across the sky?

The rocket racing for the moon?
The spaceship exploring the unknown?

Atomic power with unlimited potential?
Or the bomb — capable of destroying the world?

Man is more powerful than all his tools!

Man made the car, the jet, the rocket,
the robot, and the bomb.

Man operates every machine he has created.
Man pushes the buttons.

Without man no rocket will ever be launched.
Without man no war can begin.

Man wills to destroy himself—
or save himself.

It is all a matter of the will.

He can choose his destiny, his eternal destiny.

He puts himself into his own hands.
Or the Devil's.
Or God's.

He is given this freedom.
He is capable of choosing salvation or damnation.

Even so, it is impossible for man to save himself.
That is God's prerogative.

And since we would only bungle it,
God wants to set man free.

He offers us a new beginning.
He announces pardon.

God loves us and has given himself for us.
This alone is our salvation.

> *Like men rescued from certain death, put
> yourselves in God's hands as weapons of
> good for His own purposes. For sin is not
> meant to be your master — you are no
> longer living under the Law, but under
> grace.*
>
> **—Romans 6:13, 14**

Destruction is not meant to be.
Yours is the power of choice.

Your *will* is the most powerful instrument you
possess.

33

TO WHOM DO YOU BELONG?

A tool can be most useful.
You can use it to cut, hammer, saw, dig, or file.

But what happens when you loan a tool to your
neighbor,
and he doesn't return it?

It's yours, but you can't use it.
It still belongs to you,
but you don't possess it.

Something like this has happened to man.

Once we belonged to God.
But we've loaned ourselves out.

We chose to do that.
Now we serve ourselves.
We do not choose to serve God.

The tool is still being used.
Only by the wrong master.

"He who is without faith in Christ
is always dominated by sin" (Martin Luther).

You belong to whom you choose to obey.

We have all obeyed our sinful natures.
We have followed our own devices.

It has given us a bad taste in our mouths,
a sinking feeling in our stomachs—
and guilt.

In this condition we've probably pushed
every panic button we could think of.

Like the pilot of a jet fighter
who is forced to eject, pushing the button,
pulling the lever, or, if necessary,
prying the canopy open manually so he can get out.

Man still has another "out."

> *You belong to the power which you choose*
> *to obey, whether you choose sin, whose*
> *reward is death, or God, obedience to*
> *whom means the reward of righteousness.*
> **—Romans 6:16**

You may choose God.
You belong to whom you choose to obey.

Belonging to our rightful Owner means life.

He is our Creator.
He is our Redeemer.

The gospel is not really like
a panic button in an emergency.

But it's the only way to fly!

34

GIFTS AND PAYMENTS

The broad gate is wide open.
The narrow gate is shut.

The broad road says, "no money down."
The narrow way says, "cash on the line."

The broad way hides the price tag.
The narrow way insists that you count the cost.

The broad way beckons seductively.
The narrow way tells you no lies.

The broad road means coasting downhill.
The narrow way offers a struggle uphill.

But how do they end?
Who has looked down both roads?

The broad way ends in misery and despair.
The narrow way ends in joy and peace.

The broad way leads to destruction.
The narrow way leads to life.

The broad way closes in a narrow pit.
The narrow way opens to the wide expanse of heaven.

There is payment with interest at the end of sin.
A gift awaits us at the end of a righteous life.

The wages of sin are shame and bondage.
Yet we cannot *earn* the gift of God.

The payment is death.
The gift is life.

> **Sin pays its servants: the wage is death.
> But God gives to those who serve him: His
> free gift is eternal life through Jesus Christ
> our Lord.**
>
> **—Romans 6:23**

I heard this conversation in a diner
somewhere in New Jersey.

"What happened to Ralph?"
"He died a year ago."

"He died? No kidding!"

"Yep, he drank too much."
"Oh, yeah?"

"Yeah, he had three quarts of whiskey.
Heart attack. Drank too much."

"That's the way it goes."

"Yeah, like I always say: you might as well
go down swinging, doing what you like to do."

The only difference is that you go *down* swinging—
or you come *up* living!

35

A NEW FREEDOM

"This is a free country, and I can do as I please."

No you can't.

You can't drive down the left side of the street.
You can't carry an explosive on an airplane.

You can't help yourself to the cash at the bank.
You can't go around attacking people.

You are only free within the laws of society.
You can't do as you please.

You are no more free
than a fish out of water.

Freedom is not license.
Freedom is only freedom within certain limits.

A Christian finds freedom in the grace of God.
This means that he is freed from his sins.
He is released from his guilt.

He is liberated from the bondage of the Law.
He doesn't have to save himself any longer.

Paul illustrates this as follows:

A husband and wife are bound in marriage.

If he dies she is allowed to remarry.
The death of her husband "sets her free."

We were under the bondage of the Law.
Married to it, so to speak.

But the death of Christ has set us free.

Why?
Because the Law has been completed!
Finished . . . fulfilled.

> *The death of Christ on the Cross has made you "dead" to the claims of the Law, and you are free to give yourselves in marriage, so to speak, to Another, the One who was raised from the dead, that you may be productive for God.*
>
> **—Romans 7:4**

But this leads to a new *marriage*.
Not to the Law but to God.

A married person is not free.
He accepts a bond willingly.

He is free to be a husband.
He is not free to play the field.

If he is happily married,
he will not desire any other freedom.

A Christian is set free by the Son of God.
But he is free only as long as calls Jesus "Lord."

It's the freedom Augustine had in mind
when he summed up the Christian life like this:

"Love God and do what you will."

36

FREEDOM AND RESPONSIBILITY

Every member of an orchestra is free.
He is free to play his instrument.

But he is not free to play it whenever he wants to.
If he does the result will be a jumble of discord.

Utter confusion.
Just noise.

Only as every instrument follows
the guidance of the conductor
can there be harmony and music.

To be free in Christ means freedom under his
lordship.
He is the only One who knows how to get a melody
out of our mixed-up lives.

You cannot say "yes" to some things
without saying "no" to other things.

If you want a good figure,
you cut down on calories.

If you desire to achieve,
you stop being lazy.

You have only so much time,
limited energies, and measured abilities.

You cannot do everything.
But you can do something.

And you are free to choose.

What you do with your time is yours by choice.
What you do with your life is yours by choice.

> *We are free to serve God not in the old obedience to the letter of the Law, but in a new way, in the spirit.*
>
> **—Romans 7:6**

A member of an orchestra
is not free to play on his own.
He is part of a unit.

He executes his part according to the score.
But he is free to produce music.

The man who knows he is free
joyously responds to the Conductor.

He realizes that this is the only way
to get music out of his poor instrument.

We are free *to serve.*

37

THE AWAKENING OF SIN

A famous football coach once said,

"I have never felt that football built character.
That is done by parents and church.

You give us a boy with character,
and we will give you back a man.

You give us a character,
and we will give him right back to you."
                                    —John McKay

As football cannot build character,
so neither can the Law.

Surely the Law of God is good.
It points, lectures, and commands.

It says, "Thou shalt" and "Thou shalt not."
It awakens sin.

The Law tells me not to steal.
Now what happens?

I am suddenly made aware of stealing!
I may never have given it too much thought before.

Now I begin to wonder, "Why not?"
I ask myself, "What's wrong with it?"

The Law doesn't build my character.
It awakens the *weaknesses* of my character.

It erects a fence,

and I want to jump over that fence.

It confines me.
So I become curious.

What's on the other side of the hill?

Isn't the grass always greener over there?
Supposedly it is. . . .

> *I should never have felt guilty of the sin of coveting if I had not heard the Law saying "Thou shalt not covet." But the sin in me, finding in the commandment an opportunity to express itself, stimulated all my covetous desires.*
>
> **—Romans 7:7, 8**

The commandment which was supposed to direct me to life
turns out to be a sentence of death.

Even worse—I found out something about myself, something which I never suspected before.

And I don't like it.

Instead of liking myself,
I now find it much more difficult to accept all this.

I am actually not as good as I thought I was.
I am full of desires and motives I never knew existed.

> *The contact of the Law showed the sinful nature of sin.*
>
> **—Romans 7:13**

38

UNMASKING THE HIDDEN SELF

A man stormed into the office of his minister,
Dr. Alexander Whyte of Scotland.

An evangelist had come to Edinburgh
and had preached against the clergy.
He had said that a certain minister was not a
Christian.

"How dare he!" cried out Whyte;
"that man of God not a Christian?"

"He also said that Dr. . . . was not a Christian."

"Dr. . . .? Incredible! He's one of the finest,
most devoted men of God I know."

"And, Dr. Whyte, he also said that
you were not a Christian."

There was a moment's silence.

"Leave me, my friend," said the
sensitive and committed minister;
"I want to be alone.
I must examine myself."

This same Alexander Whyte says that
Paul is both the most consistent and the most
inconsistent of all Christ's converts.

The most blameless and the most blamable.
The best-proportioned and the most disproportioned.

The honesty of the Christian is

nowhere better presented than in Romans 7.

Here is the struggle of a free man
who has awakened to his inherent sinfulness.

His true nature lies revealed.
Sin still dwells within.
The struggle to be a Christian is tearing him apart.

> *My own behavior baffles me. For I find
> myself not doing what I really want to do
> but doing what I really loathe. Yet surely
> if I do things that I really don't want to do,
> it cannot be said that "I" am doing them at
> all—it must be sin that has made its home
> in my nature. . . . I often find that I have
> the will to do good but not the power.*
> **—Romans 7:15-18**

Many a Christian would be swallowed up by despair
had it not been for this honest, forthright man named
Paul.

Or for saintly ministers like Alexander Whyte.

Christians know that their salvation lies not in
themselves.
Self-examination only reveals their need for Christ.

Our wills are not enough.
The power must come from Above.

39

THE GREATEST TRAGEDY OF ALL

Tragic as Macbeth, Hamlet, King Lear, and Othello
are, they are but staged tragedies.

Great as they are,
the tragedy of Paul seems greater.

Here is a man caught in the awful maze of sin.
He attempts to be a Christian.

He is locked in a fierce battle with himself.
Heaven and hell meet within his soul.

He describes himself as physically tied to a corpse.

Death and life are bound together—
sin *and* the desire for the holy.

No man experiences this,
but he who is on the way to God.

No man knows what this is all about,
but he who is awakened by the Spirit.

No man testifies to this,
but one who has set out to be a Christian.

"I don't think I had any real knowledge of my own
sinfulness
until long after I had become a Christian" (Eileen
Guder).

In my mind I am God's willing servant,
but in my own nature I am bound fast, as I

say, to the law of sin and death. It is an agonizing situation, and who on earth can set me free from the clutches of my own sinful nature? I thank God there is a way out through Jesus Christ our Lord.
—Romans 7:22-25

But this tragedy does not end tragically.
It ends victoriously.

The heroes of Shakespeare lose their lives in despair.
They are indeed tragic heroes.

Jesus died on a bitter cross.
But He knew his way out of the tomb!
He triumphed over death.

Christians will reach the promised land.
They follow One who has already arrived.

Tragedy has turned to victory!

40

THE GREATEST VICTORY OF ALL

There is an old fable about the wind and the sun.
They argued with one another about which was the
stronger.

The wind tried to blow a coat off a man.
But it failed.

Then the sun sweated if off with plenty of heat!

What the cold Law could not accomplish with its
commands,
the warmth of Christ's love could.

In spite of the frankness of Romans 7,
there is no failure in Romans 8.

In spite of Paul's honesty about his inner self,
his life in Christ has the ring of victory.

> *No condemnation now hangs over the*
> *head of those who are "in" Jesus Christ.*
> *For the new spiritual principle of life "in"*
> *Christ lifts me out of the old vicious circle*
> *of sin and death.*
>
> **—Romans 8:1**

Is it normal to think of defeat instead of victory?

Will evil conquer good?
Will Satan triumph over God?

Will Christ be ultimately dethroned?
Whose kingdom will come?

Whose will shall be done on earth, as it is in heaven?

We do not expect to live sick lives.
We expect health.

Sickness is not the normal.
Health is the normal.

We fall into sin, just as we may get sick.
But recovery is our goal.

We are sinners, that is true.
But Christ has redeemed us—that is also true.

Sin dwells within.
But so does the Spirit of God.

We ought not to expect a sinsick life.
We ought to expect to be healthy Christians.

Jesus does not even want us to be anemic.
He wants us to be completely whole.

Ultimate defeat is abnormal.
You may expect victory!

41

FLESH AND SPIRIT

Skid row is filled with broken men.
Men without a goal.
Men who lack purpose.

Men who refused authority.
Men who neglected discipline.

Helpless men.
Hopeless men.

Men do not rise to the top by doing as they please.

A soldier does not become a general by giving orders.
He takes orders.
He submits to authority.

The stronger the man,
the more necessary the controls.

Man would be destructive without them.

Only a productive man knows how to
channel his resources.

Only a submissive man knows how to
rule his own spirit.

Life in the Spirit is like that.

It can never succeed by refusing authority.
It can only succeed by submission.

The stronger my will,
the greater my need for the Spirit of God.

The more rebellious my flesh,
the greater my need for Spirit-control.

Sin is not extracted like a tooth.
It is counteracted by God's Spirit.

Like a disease, treated with progressive medication.
Like a cancer, burned away with continuous
treatment.

Like fear, finally overcome by courage.
Like hatred, counteracted by steady love.
Like pride, downed by ever-present humility.

> *The carnal attitude sees no further than*
> *natural things. But the spiritual attitude*
> *reaches out after the things of the spirit.*
> *The former attitude means, bluntly, death,*
> *the latter means life and inward peace. . . .*
> *You are not carnal but spiritual if the*
> *Spirit of God finds a home within you. You*
> *cannot, indeed, be a Christian at all unless*
> *you have something of His Spirit in you.*
> **—Romans 8:6, 9**

What was managed from below
is now controlled from above.

What was once merely flesh
has now the added dimension of the Spirit.

The man who refuses authority will end up broken.
But the man who is willing to be broken now
will finish in triumph!

42

INSTINCT?

Can the Spirit of God make a fundamental change in your life?

Or do you think that people are mainly types, and that types can't be changed?

You know, the introvert and the extrovert.
The easygoing type.
The melancholy type.
The worried type.
The glamorous type.
The depressive type.

Do you think that most people live according to instinct?
(Instinct is supposed to be a woman's big asset!)

If true, would this eliminate any need for divine direction?

Can we manage it all nicely ourselves?
Just follow our instincts?
Make the most of our types?

"Doing what comes naturally?"

Why not?
Aren't we supposed to maneuver on our own?

As a matter of fact many believe this.

They do believe vaguely in Almighty God.
They believe to some extent in Jesus of Nazareth.

But as far as the Holy Spirit is concerned,
that's not on their program.

They can do without that.
They don't understand it.

The Holy Spirit?
Why is that necessary?
What's the point?

But there is a pessimism attached to being typed.

What if you're the wrong type?
Then what chance do you have?

What if you possess a poor instinct?
Then what?

For a better world you need better people.
To get better people you need ideals and faith.

But you need even more:

> *You can see that we have no particular*
> *reason to feel grateful to our instinctive*
> *nature, or to live life on the level of the in-*
> *stincts. Indeed, that way of living leads to*
> *certain spiritual death. But if on the other*
> *hand you cut the nerve of your instinctive*
> *actions by obeying the Spirit, you are on*
> *the way to real living.*
> **—Romans 8:12, 13**

God works through all types!
His Spirit lives in you.

And that's really much better
than relying on your instinct.

43

COMING BACK HOME

A little girl and her brother boarded a bus.

"I want two tickets to Hamilton," she said,
"And two to come back."

"So you want to come back?" asked the driver.

"Yes, we want to come back," she said.
She emphasized *we want to.*

He punched the tickets and replied,
"If you want to come back, why are you going
away?"

So we start our journey in life.

We take a trip into the far country.
We choose our masters.

We get away from God.
But we want to be able to return home.

The far country isn't all it's supposed to be.
The publicity is overdone.

The posters told lies.
The advertisers oversold their product.

Only too late we discover we've been duped.

It's good to know that we can come home.

Our Father allowed us to leave,
although He didn't want us to go.

Even while we were away
He never forgot us.

We were missing from the family circle.
It was incomplete.

When we return, however hesitatingly,
He receives us with open arms.

He's been waiting for us all the time.

And He doesn't hold it against us.
He knows our frailty.

He does not excuse us.
But He does forgive us.

He does not overlook our guilt.
But He does justify the guilty.

And He will not bring up the subject again,
no matter how much we have hurt Him.

We are really back in the family—back home.

> *You have been adopted into the very family circle of God and you can say with a full heart, "Father, my Father." The Spirit Himself endorses our inward conviction that we really are the children of God.*
>
> **—Romans 8:15, 16**

Even those who were in the clutches of their own sinful nature
can live with this assurance.

106

Even those who despaired in the far country may once again come home.

That's good news.
We are *actually* His children.

44

OUR MAGNIFICENT FUTURE

Sir Thomas More never for a moment
lost sight of the goal.

No matter what forces were arrayed against him,
he remained faithful to God.

He was not blinded by the glare of victory.
He was not dejected by the cloud of defeat.

This man for all seasons moved steadily
toward the truth before him.

He was not afraid to hold to his own belief,
even against the king's demands.

He could not endorse the king's divorce
and his desire to remarry.

God alone was God for him.

When he was told of the king's wrath
and his own impending death, he said,

"Then in good faith there is no more difference
between Your Grace and me, but that I shall die
today
and you tomorrow."

What does it mean to be a member of God's family?
What does it mean in the face of death?

The family to which we belong is eternal.
Relationships cannot be broken.

God is our *Father*.
What He has planned for man is beyond our comprehension.

And that means our battle is worthwhile.
We need not despair.
The most hopeless situation is not the final chapter.

We cannot rise from the pits into which we stumble by sheer human effort.

We are enabled to get out *only because* there is something better ahead.

We live in hope.

> *In my opinion whatever we may have to go through now is less than nothing compared with the magnificent future God has planned for us. . . . Hope always means waiting for something that we haven't yet got. But if we hope for something we cannot see, then we must settle down to wait for it in patience.*
> **—Romans 8:18, 25**

Living by hope is better than despair.

Keeping your eye on the future is better than relinquishing to your evil nature.

Know your magnificent future!

God is not only God.
God is *your Father*.

45

FAITH AND CIRCUMSTANCE

As a very young lawyer Daniel Webster was given an insurance case for which he received only $25.

He had to make a trip to Boston for his client.
He knew he would never be reimbursed for it.

He took the trip anyway.
He had to consult the law library in Boston.

Because of this sacrificial effort, he won the case.

Years later Webster, now famous, was traveling through New York.

An important insurance company asked him to substitute for a lawyer who had become ill.

Money was no object, they said.

Webster explained that he could not possibly prepare such a case in a few hours.

They insisted that he look at it.
As he did so, he discovered his old $25 case.

He had not forgotten it.
Because of that trip to Boston, he was ready to step in now.

He won the case and received a handsome fee.

Not everything will be rewarded like that.
Nor will it come out that smoothly.

But even in our most trying circumstances,
we may be assured that there is a plan:

> *We know that to those who love God, who
> are called according to His plan,
> everything that happens fits into a pattern
> for good. God, in his foreknowledge,
> chose them to bear the family likeness of
> His Son.*
>
> **—Romans 8:28, 29**

We know, so we need not fear.
We believe, so we need not doubt.

Everything fits—not just a few things.
It really *fits*—it is not lost in an unsolvable puzzle.

It is a pattern, not a mishmash.
It is for good, because we belong to His family.

God engineers it.
These are not merely circumstances.

In view of these *facts*,
what else do we need to know?

46

PROMISES, PROMISES

We have been told that nations offer paper promises.

They sound good on paper,
but they are never actually adhered to.

Unbreakable watches can be broken.
Lifetime pens run out of ink.
And the insurance company does not always pay.

Marriages launched with the promise
"till death us do part" often end up in divorce.

What of the promises of God?

Are they only good on paper—even though it is
Biblical paper?

Are they make-believe, metaphors, fairy tales?

Or are they fact—reality—truth?

Is it arrogance on our part to believe these promises?
Is it pride to hope for their fulfillment?

Or can we humbly trust them?

God's promises will only be valid if

1) some *have been* fulfilled;
2) some *will be* fulfilled.

Some *have been* fulfilled.

Old Testament promises were fulfilled in the New
Testament.

Predictions of the Messiah were fulfilled by Jesus.

Sprinkled all through the New Testament
are quotes from the Old.

> *There shall come out of Zion the
> Deliverer; He shall turn away ungodliness
> from Jacob: And this is my covenant unto
> them, When I shall take away their sins.*
> **—Romans 11:26, 27**

Some *will yet be* fulfilled.

Promises of the kingdom—when it comes.
Promises of eternity—when we enter it.

There is only one way we can believe promises.

Not by building dream castles.
Not by empty hopes.
Not by mere imagination.

But on the certainty of the good news.
By submitting to the Word of God.

> *In face of all this, what is there left to say?
> If God is for us, who can be against us? He
> that did not hesitate to spare His own Son,
> but gave Him up for us all—can we not
> trust such a God to give us, with Him,
> everything else that we can need?*
> **—Romans 8:31, 32**

They are, after all, the promises of *God*!

114

47

ABSOLUTELY CONVINCED

If a Christian could avoid all trouble, suffering, and tragedy,
everyone would become a Christian.

If immunity was a guarantee,
the world would jump on the Christian bandwagon.

But that would hardly be a worthy motive.

Christians are *not* immune.

They also must face danger, accident, cancer, and death.

They too will be tempted to ask,
"Why did God allow this to happen to me?"

The Bible does not promise us sanctuary from suffering.

We may not be spared a coronary
or the death of an only son.

To the contrary.

Through suffering we gain insight
into our reason for being.

Through suffering we may also learn
the inseparable power of God's love.

No one can merely tell us about it.
We must experience it ourselves.

Nothing can shake us loose from God.
Nothing can come between.

Not the fear of death or the trials of life.
Not the past or the future.
Not all the powers that be.

A woman came to her minister with an objection:
"I can't trust *myself*," she said.

But *we* are covered also.
We may be faithless, but He remains faithful.

We are held in His hand.
We are His beloved children.

> *I have become absolutely convinced that neither death nor life, neither messenger of heaven nor monarch of earth, neither what happens today nor what may happen tomorrow, neither a power from on high nor a power from below, nor anything else in God's whole world has any power to separate us from the love of God in Jesus Christ our Lord!*
> **—Romans 8:38, 39**

A great Christian who had gone through many trials asked for his Bible while on his deathbed.

When they opened it for him to Romans 8,
he put his finger on it and died in peace.

Absolutely convinced.

PART IV

SOLVING PROBLEMS OF FAITH

"God's thoughts, his will, his love, his
judgments are all man's home.
To think his thoughts, to choose his will,
to love his loves, to judge his judgments,
and thus to know that he is in us,
is to be at home."

—George Macdonald

48

A PACKAGE DEAL

Bob Hope was in flight over the Alps,
and the going was rough.

They had to fasten their seat belts,
and the passengers became frightened.

At the height of the battle with the wind
a soldier bowed his head in prayer.

Bob Hope spoke up:
"Make it a package deal. Include all of us."

Moses made it a package deal.
He prayed for his people.

And he was even willing to have himself
excluded from the package for the sake of his nation.

Paul made it a package deal.
He prayed for his fellow Israelites.

He saw them without the good news.
They did not believe in Jesus.

He prayed so fervently for them
that he also excluded himself.

> *Before Christ and my own conscience I*
> *assure you that I am speaking the plain*
> *truth when I say that there is something*
> *that makes me feel very depressed, like a*
> *pain that never leaves me. It is the con-*
> *dition of my brothers and fellow-*

*Israelites, and I have actually reached the
pitch of wishing myself cut off from Christ
if it meant that they could be won for God.*
—Romans 9:1-3

Jesus did not pray only for His people,
nor did He merely weep over the city of Jerusalem.

He sacrificed Himself for Israel
and for all the world.

He moved from prayer to action.
He was made sin, He who knew no sin.

He was willing to be forsaken of God
to bring us to God.

And because of Jesus' sacrifice,
whoever will may come.

It *is* a package deal!

49

PRIVILEGE AND RESPONSIBILITY

You have a body.
You can allow it to become soft and flabby.
Or you can keep it athletic.
But that will require continuous exercise.

You have a mind.

You can let others do your thinking for you.
Or you can think for yourself.

You can swallow predigested entertainment.
Or you can exert mental effort and do some thinking.

You have other gifts.

You can hide them.
Or you can put them to use.

You can bury them.
Or you can plant them.

You can say, "Let George do it."
But why let George have all the glory?

With privilege goes responsibility.

Just think what the Israelites have had given to them. The privilege of being adopted as sons of God, the experience of seeing something of the glory of God, the receiving of the agreements made with God, the gift of the Law, true ways of worship, God's own promises ... and so too, as far as human descent goes, is Christ Himself.

—**Romans 9:4, 5**

Israel had all the advantages.
Israel did not accept responsibility.

Through Israel came the Savior of the world.
But they refused to believe their Messiah.

They still remain ignorant
of their greatest gift to the world.

You have great privileges.
But they become responsibilities.

Don't bury your life.
Plant it.

50

NATURAL AND SPIRITUAL

When a famous Hebrew leader came to Jesus he was
told, "You must be born anew."

It was a completely new idea to Nicodemus.
He had never thought about it.

Born anew?
Born spiritually?
Born from above?
Why?

He was a Jew.
The Jews were God's chosen people, weren't they?
He was a son of Abraham, wasn't he?

Was not every Jew acceptable to God?

Why need he be reborn?
Was it not enough to have been born a Jew?

At a junior high camp a boy gave this definition
of a Christian:

"A Christian is an American."

What had his parents taught him?
It smacks of superiority.

We are a God-fearing nation.
We are God's chosen people.

God did not choose the Russians or the Chinese.
He chose Americans.

Day Brighteners from Romans

Our founding fathers were religious.
We alone started this nation under God.

No one else has a Declaration of Independence.

Washington was our father.
Jefferson was our genius.
Lincoln brought us through the Red Sea of slavery.

We are a Christian people.
Why need we be reborn?

We are already in the favor of Providence.
We are his chosen representatives on earth.

> *You cannot count all "Israelites" as the true Israel of God. . . . It is not the natural descendants who automatically inherit the promise, but, on the contrary, the children of the promise (i.e., the sons of God) are to be considered truly Abraham's children.*
> **—Romans 9:6, 8**

Obviously there's a little more to it.
What, after all, makes you a Christian?

Unless you are spiritually reborn
you will never see the kingdom of God.

51

GOD'S CHOICE AND MAN'S FREEDOM

God makes choices.
We may wonder why.

Why was I born white, yellow, or black?
Why was I born in America, Asia, or Africa?
Why was I born to a wealthy family or in a slum?

That choice is fixed on me from the beginning.
I cannot do anything about it.

There are no answers for such questions.

Abraham had several children.
But only one son was his true descendant.

Ishmael was sent into the desert with his mother.
His later sons were not considered rightful heirs.

Abraham gave all that he had to Isaac.
Isaac received the promises.

Isaac became the father of twin boys.
But before they were born a choice had been made.

God made that choice.
God predicted that Jacob would receive the promises.
The other son (Esau) would be rejected.

> *It came before the children were born or
> had done anything good or bad, plainly
> showing that God's act of choice has
> nothing to do with achievements, good or*

*bad, but is entirely a matter of His will.
. . . Jacob I loved, but Esau I hated.*

—Romans 9:11, 13

How is this possible?
Is it fair?

How can God be said to hate Esau?
And even *before* he was born?

God knows the end from the beginning.
He knows how we will turn out.

By foreknowledge He announces who will receive the promise
and who will reject it.

On what basis?
Because He is partial?
Because He loves one and despises another?
Because He will not give Esau a chance?

Not so!

Man is free to choose his destiny.
Or else he would be a puppet.

God is not fate.
Man's life is not predetermined.

Man is free to act.
But God knows *how* he will act.

God knows the choices we will make.
On that basis He announces our actions beforehand.

The real problem is not with "Esau I hated."
It is with "Jacob I loved."

How could God love this deceptive, cunning Jacob?
How could God love anyone like us?

In spite of everything, Jacob chose God.
He repented in earnest.

God damns no one to hell.
We damn only ourselves.

52

THE DIVINE MERCY

A medical student hated his father.
His father made him study hard.
He was constantly driving him on.

The night before his graduation
his father explained something.

Years earlier his health had seriously failed.
The doctor had warned him.
He had been told to give up working.

The father decided to remain in business
for his son's sake.

He prayed that he might live
to see his son graduate.

When the son realized this, he hated no longer.
He saw his father in a new light.

We may not understand everything about God.
But we believe He is our heavenly Father.

How do you think of God?

Is He a policeman who spoils your fun?
Ready to pull you over to the curb
to hand you a ticket for your sins?

Or is He like a grandfather
who leniently gives cookies to his good children?

Is God harsh and cruel, destructive or wrathful?

Ready to smash you down at the judgment?

Is God a heavenly bosom on which you may lean for comfort,
to help you through tough times?

Or has He let you down when it really mattered?
Is He a disappointment to you?

Is God fair or unfair?
Just or unjust?

How do you see God?

> *Now do we conclude that God is monstrously unfair? Never! God said long ago to Moses, "I will have mercy on whom I have mercy, and I will have compassion on whom I have compassion." . . . God chooses on whom He will have mercy, and whom He will harden in their sin.*
> **—Romans 9:14, 15, 18**

However you may think of God,
let Scripture correct your faulty opinions.

God is your *Father*,
and He is compassionate!

53

WHY? WHY? WHY?

Of course I can almost hear your retort: "If this is so, and God's will is irresistible, why does God blame men for what they do?" But the question really is this: "Who are you, a man, to make any such reply to God?"

—Romans 9:19, 20

God is not on trial.
He runs the world according to his will.

He is sovereign.
Who are we to judge him?

We are not the critics of God.
He is our Critic.

The problem is never with a holy God.
It is always with sinful men.

The problem is not with a compassionate Father.
It is always with rebellious sons.

The miracle is not that God rejects sinners.
The miracle is that God has not destroyed the world.

The question is not "Why does God blame man?"
The question is "Why does man blame God?"

We ask the wrong questions.
We seek the wrong solutions.

We blame the world without.

We will not look within.

Our questions point away from ourselves.
Our accusations are turned on God.

It is camouflage to ask "Why?"
It would be more honest to ask "What?"

When we ask "Why did God allow this?"
we divert ourselves from action.

When we ask "What can I do now?"
we discover some of the answers.

Only when we trust him as our Father.
Only when we commit ourselves to Him.
Only when we come to know Him.

That means turning on ourselves in repentance.
That means trusting Him in faith.

It's the only way light will break into our darkness.

> *The potter, for instance, is always assumed to have complete control over the clay, making with one part of the lump a lovely vase, and with another a pipe for sewage. Can we not assume that God has the same control over human clay?*
> **—Romans 9:21**

God is not on trial.
We are.

54

MAGIC GLASSES

There's an old story by George William Curtis.
It's about a pair of glasses.

Magic glasses.
When their owner put them on, he could
see through any person to the real man inside.

He looked through one man and saw a bank.
He looked through another and saw a bottle.
He looked through a third and saw a book.

What is man?
What does he look like?

He is free to choose his life.

But there is one characteristic common to us all.
Sin is rooted in our freedom.

We want to write our own script.
We will not adhere to the Script which is written.

We want to run our lives our own way.
We are fighting against God.

That's what it's all about.

We will not simply believe the good news.
We want to achieve our own salvation.

We will not come humbly to Christ.
We want to make our own way to God.

Our real kick is always *against* something.

Or Someone.

But what good is it to be merely *against*?
Is that enough of a challenge?

Why not be *for* something?
For Someone!

> *Israel, following the Law of righteousness,*
> *failed to reach the goal of righteousness.*
> *And why? Because their minds were fixed*
> *on what they achieved instead of on what*
> *they believed. . . . All the time they are*
> *going about trying to prove their own*
> *righteousness—they have the wrong at-*
> *titude to receive His.*
> **—Romans 9:31, 32; 10:3**

Why not live for that which God created us?
And for which Christ died?

What if someone were to look at you with magic
glasses?
What would he find?

55

THE SECRET OF FAITH

When an artist paints a picture,
he does not make it up out of his head.

He observes a still life.
He interprets what he sees.

He watches a person and paints his portrait.

When a poet writes a poem,
he draws out of nature what is already there.

Just as there is a world around us,
which few of us ever really observe—

So there is an Eternal World,
which many fail to recognize.

Only the man of faith sees it bombarding our shores.
He hears it splashing upon us from the Beyond.

He knows that the invisible world is a real world,
since an invasion has taken place.

The Eternal has pierced time.
The Word was made flesh
and dwelt among us.

Christ has come into the here and now.

On this solid fact we build our faith.
Not on what we vainly hope may be true.

Not on imagination.
Not on fantasy.

But on what we have observed in Christ.

Faith is not apprehending some truth about God.
Faith is knowing the reality of God.

Faith is not reaching into the unknown.
Faith is receiving the unknown in the known Christ.

Faith is not studying and learning.
(Nor can learning become a substitute for faith!)

Faith is man's response to God's gift.
Faith is being certain of things we cannot see.

Faith is the relationship which is established
through the revelation of Christ.

It is trust in the truth.

> *The secret of faith . . . says, in effect, "If
> you openly admit by your own mouth that
> Jesus Christ is the Lord, and if you believe
> in your own heart that God raised Him
> from the dead, you will be saved." . . .
> Whosoever shall call upon the name of the
> Lord shall be saved.*
>
> **—Romans 10:9, 13**

Anyone can have faith.
Anyone can believe the good news.

56

THE NECESSITY OF RESPONSE

A child sees what he sees.
An adult sees what he knows.

Adults interpret everything they see.
It's all according to past experience.

The child humbly accepts.
He sees what he actually sees.

Can we become childlike in this?

> *Now how can they call on One in whom*
> *they have never believed? How can they*
> *believe in One of whom they have never*
> *heard?*
>
> **—Romans 10:14**

Someone wrote to the Russian writer Turgenev,

"It seems to me that to put yourself in second place
is the whole significance of life."

Replied Turgenev,

"It seems to me that to discover
what one should put in the first place
is the whole problem of life."

Whom shall we believe in childlike faith?

You remain unhappy unless you will accept
the condition for happiness.

It is a matter of response.

Not reaction.

> *Yet all who have heard have not responded to the gospel. Isaiah asks, you remember, "Lord, who hath believed our report?"*
>
> **—Romans 10:16**

Belief is receiving.
Belief is responding.

Belief is action.
Belief is surrender.

Does a child lose everything when he
listens wholeheartedly to a teacher?

Does a man act foolishly when he
submits himself completely to his physician?

Must we always analyze?
Or dare we simply believe?

> *Belief, you see, can only come from hearing the message, and the message is the word of Christ.*
>
> **—Romans 10:17**

God does not present us with a supposition.
He gives us a message.

It is better to accept that message
than to continue in everlasting analysis.

It's better to accept it
than to hold our faulty opinions.

57

GOD AND ISRAEL

The first disciples were Jews.
The earliest Christians were Jews.

All the New Testament authors (except one)
were Jews.

It took some doing on the part of God
to move these Christian Jews into the Gentile world!

Finally Peter received a special vision.
And he obeyed it, but reluctantly.

Throughout history Jews have become Christians.

Composers like Mendelssohn and Offenbach.
The poet Da Costa.

The painter Rosa Bonheur.
The actress Sarah Bernhardt.

The news pioneer Baron Reuter.
Joseph Pulitzer, the editor.
Benjamin Disraeli, prime minister of England.

"Christians may continue to persecute Jews,
and Jews may persist in disbelieving Christians—

But who can deny that Jesus of Nazareth,
the incarnate Son of the most high God,
is the eternal glory of the Jewish race?"

So wrote Disraeli.

Yet it is not the noble or the mighty whom God
calls—
it is the foolish who will confound the wise.

Not many famous Jews are on that roll.
But there are some who have believed in Jesus.

There are Jewish Christians today.
They think of themselves as completed Jews.
They have found their Messiah.

They may not be famous.
But their names are written in the book of life.

> *Has God then totally repudiated His
> people? Certainly not! I myself, for one,
> am an Israelite, a descendant of Abraham
> and of the tribe of Benjamin. It is un-
> thinkable that God should have
> repudiated His own people, the people
> whose destiny He Himself appointed.*
> **—Romans 11:1, 2**

God has never left himself without a witness.
There has always been a nucleus—
even from His own people.

The good news will never be *totally* rejected.

58

GOD'S PURPOSES IN FAILURE

Whistler wanted to become a soldier,
but he failed at West Point.

Reluctantly he turned to painting.

Scott wanted to be a poet.
He gave it up since he could never equal Byron.

He was so ashamed of writing a novel
that he did it anonymously.
But he gave us *Ivanhoe*.

As a boy Glenn Cunningham was badly burned.
His doctor thought he would remain an invalid.

Cunningham changed his destiny.
He became a world champion mile runner.

Phillips Brooks wanted to teach.
He failed.

He turned to preaching
and became one of the world's greatest preachers.

Israel failed to acknowledge the Messiah,
to respond to the good news.

But God used that failure to great advantage.
The whole world would hear the gospel.

The early Christians always went first
into the synagogues.

When their message was rejected,

they were forced into the streets.

To the Jew first—then to the Gentile.

> *Now I ask myself, "Was this fall of theirs*
> *an utter disaster?" It was not! For through*
> *their failure the benefit of salvation has*
> *passed to the Gentiles, with the result that*
> *Israel is made to see and feel what it has*
> *missed.*
>
> **—Romans 11:11**

Israel missed the very thing it had been looking for.
Israel missed the best part. . . .

It's not been worth it.
But even so it's not too late.

Not for them.
Not for anyone.
Not for you!

God can always bring success out of failure.

59

DO YOU FEEL SUPERIOR?

"My father is stronger than your father."

"But my father can beat up your father."

"Oh yeah?"
"Yeah."

That's children for you.

"My car is bigger than your car."

"My house is better than your house."

"My job is higher than your job."

That's adults for you.

"I am above you socially.
I make more than you do.
Therefore I won't have anything to do with you."

Some Christians feel superior too.
"My religion is better than your religion."

Christians can never boast before the Jews.
For this is what has really happened:

God planted a tree.
This tree was Israel.

The roots of it were dedicated to Him
(Abraham, Isaac, Jacob, Joseph).

Every branch of the tree belongs to Him.

But some branches were broken off.
That made room for a wild olive tree to be grafted in.

The Gentiles are like this wild olive tree.

They are allowed to share in the natural tree.

And that is hardly ground for superiority!

The Jews were broken off because of unbelief.
Christians maintain their position by faith.

That's no reason to feel proud.
There's a better perspective:

> *You must try to appreciate both the kindness and the strict justice of God. Those who fell experienced His justice, while you are experiencing His kindness, and will continue to do so as long as you do not abuse that kindness. Otherwise you too will be cut off from the tree.*
> **—Romans 11:22**

Besides, one of these days the natural branches will be grafted back in!

That is what God declares.

Don't boast, you former wild olive tree.
By the grace of God you are *in*.

Be thankful for that.
And stop feeling superior.

Conceit always slams the door on God.

60

THE UNCHANGING GOD

Man is always running away from God.
But he runs to other gods.

He does not want to face the living God.
Therefore he seeks out gods that seem harmless.

Modern man exhanged the glory of God
for his worldly pursuits.

But secretly he knows that God made him.
And God is eternally *there*.

American scientists made an interesting report.

They said that at top-level international scientific
discussions,
Russian scientists asked them about God.

What did the Americans believe about God?
What about spiritual resources for daily living?

Man is hooked.
The cards are stacked against him.
He has to *know*.

Is there a true God?

God has not only made us, but He loves us.
He will still have us, though we may not want Him.

He still loves us, though we follow other gods.

He remains unchanging.
Even though we keep changing our allegiance.

This is how He feels toward his children.

One son (Israel) has rebelled and left home.
In spite of his rebellion he will be welcomed back.

He cannot escape God forever.
He remains in the loving hands of God.

> *All Israel will be saved. . . . As far as God's*
> *purpose in choosing is concerned, they are*
> *still beloved for their fathers' sakes. For*
> *once they are made, God does not*
> *withdraw His gifts or His calling.*
> **—Romans 11:26, 28, 29**

God does not change.
He is the same yesterday, today, and forever.

He is always there,
in spite of our frantic, idolatrous pursuits.

"Change and decay in all around I see;
O thou who changest not, abide with me."

61

COLORED TISSUE PAPER

There's a child's puzzle.
It is a tangle of red and blue lines.
You can't make anything out of it.

But take a piece of red tissue paper.
Hold it over the puzzle, and the red lines disappear.
The blue lines make a picture of a clown.

Put blue tissue paper over it.
The blue lines disappear.
The red lines make a picture of a lion.

It all depends on the colored tissue paper.

Do we all look at the world
through our own colored tissue paper?

Some people say that things just happen.
Christians say that God is at work.

Some believe in a chain of events.
Some believe in nothing.
Christians confess that there is a Cause.

Some shrug their shoulders at circumstances.
Christians see a higher Will.

If *God* is, there is a will of God.
If God wills, there must be a sovereign purpose.

All are included in that purpose.
Jews and Christians.
And all the rest of the world.

It is a matter of faith.

It may all depend on the color of the tissue,
but faith is better than critical unbelief.

How can you rely on a God who is not in charge?
Or One who bungles the government of the universe?

A God who is not sovereign cannot be trusted.

Who can explain God?
Who can know God's plans in detail?

Who dares contain the Eternal by his finite mind?
And who can expound His purpose?

Man can only wonder and worship.
He can only pray and praise.

He can only believe—and love.

In view of the fact that he knows so little,
that is his best posture!

> *Frankly, I stand amazed at the unfathomable complexity of God's wisdom and God's knowledge. How could man ever understand His reasons for action, or explain His methods of working? For, "Who hath known the mind of the Lord?"*
>
> **—Romans 11:33, 34**

By faith you can get a better picture of God.

Actually, the only true picture.

PART V

SOLVING PROBLEMS OF LIVING

"To be like Christ
is to be a Christian."
—William Penn

62

WITH EYES WIDE OPEN

A Roman Catholic wrote a letter about Protestants.

"I'd like to tell you," he wrote *Time* Magazine,
"why Roman Catholics become converts to
Protestantism.

It's because it's so much easier
to lie abed Sunday mornings than to go to mass;

because the practice of birth control allows one
to spend one's income on oneself;

because divorce is so convenient
when you're tired of your spouse and fancy a change;
because it's nice not to have to fast during Lent."

If you are a Protestant, why are you one?
Because it's easier?

What does it mean to live as a Christian?
Is this letter a right evaluation of *Christianity*?

Does Jesus make no demands of us?

> *With eyes wide open to the mercies of*
> *God, I beg you, my brothers, as an act of*
> *intelligent worship, to give Him your*
> *bodies as a living sacrifice, consecrated to*
> *Him and acceptable by Him.*
> **—Romans 12:1**

To give?
Consecrated?

Christian living is not a snap.
Not if all this is involved.

What are we to commit?
Our bodies.

Christians generally say,
"Be spiritual. Save your soul."

But God is not asking only for our souls.
He is also asking for our bodies.

Why?

Because we are not merely spirits who have a body.
We are *persons*—body, soul, and spirit.

We cannot worship God with our spirits
and forget about our bodies.

Jesus wants us wholeheartedly.
Through our bodies we express our total selves.

Christianity is more than we make it out to be.

It means commitment.
A living sacrifice.

The motive for commitment is God's mercy.
The aim of commitment is God's service.

And all of this with eyes wide open!

63

WITH MINDS RENEWED

A sociologist views our world as a puppet show.

Each puppet runs around on stage
with a key in its back.

The keys wind them up, make them move,
and control them.

Are we all puppets of our society?

The world wants everyone to act alike.
Behave alike.
Think alike too.

Like the cans on the supermarket shelf
carrying company labels.

Conformed to the same size.
Only an oddball looks or sounds different.

Everybody else lives in the same tract homes.
Same size gardens.
With green lawns out front.

Talks about the same things.
Wears similar clothes.
Has the same hairdos.
Uses similar cosmetics.
Holds similar goals.
Does not dare to be different.

Children at school are kept at the same level.
All look alike at graduation.

And yet, no girl would be caught wearing
her grandmother's dress to a party.

Why are we satisfied to be squeezed
into the same molds?
Like products that come off an assembly line?

> *Don't let the world around you squeeze
> you into its own mold, but let God remold
> your minds from within, so that you may
> prove in practice that the plan of God for
> you is good, meets all His demands, and
> moves towards the goal of true maturity.*
> **—Romans 12:2**

If only we can look over our shoulders and *see*
those keys in our backs, we can be freed of them.

God doesn't want puppets.
He wants free men.

He is not interested in assembly-line products.
He wants us to develop into our unique potential.

Isn't that far better?

Besides, your faith should be your own.
Don't be satisfied with your grandmother's.

It may have been real for her.
It ought to be real for you, too.

64

THE GIFT OF HUMILITY

Think big.
But don't get a big head.

Do you pat yourself on the back?
Do you think you're the greatest?

Or do you have an inferiority complex?
Do you think of yourself as worthless, no good?

Either view spells disaster!

A young woman was in a Christian discussion group.
They were discussing the sins of the world.

"Of course we wouldn't ever do anything like that,"
she said.

If we hold to the illusion that we are virtuous,
we are not candidates for the grace of God.

Some Christians don't really believe
they need the forgiveness of God!

You are without question a sinner.
You have fallen short of God's ideal.

You have rebelled against Him.
It was necessary for Christ to die.
He died because of your (our) sins.

How then can you pat yourself on the back?
How can you think you're the greatest?

But. . .

You are a *forgiven* sinner!
You have been received as a child of God!

You are an heir with Christ.
You have been accepted.

Why then do you still feel inferior?
Why do you consider yourself worthless?

Christ died for you.
You belong to Him.

Think soberly.
Think realistically.

> ***Don't cherish exaggerated ideas of
> yourself or your importance, but try to
> have a sane estimate of your capabilities
> by the light of the faith that God has given
> to you all.***
> **—Romans 12:3**

God does not admire your character.
Nor does He approve of all you have done.

But He accepts you as you are.
He loves the real you.

That "you"—once innocent.
That "you"—now bleeding because of your sins.
That "you"—with the promise of perfection.

If you believe God, you cannot retain a false
view of yourself.
You will not be proud.
Nor will you bemoan your inferiority.

You will become *humble* in the right sense of the
word.

156

65

GENUINE CHRISTIANS

Christianity is not essentially *doing*.
It is rather *being*.

It is not merely acting.
It is primarily relating.

People aren't always interested in explanation.
They look for demonstration.

What will it matter if you have done some good
but failed to become the person you hoped to be?

Will wonderful works avail at the judgment?
Won't the question be, "Do you know Christ?"

Many will boast of their achievements.
Few will acknowledge the grace of God.

This grace renews a person.
This grace produces genuine Christians.

How can you get good oranges from a tree
unless you first have a fruit-bearing tree?

When you have a good tree,
you will also grow good oranges.

When you envision the person Christ wants you to become,
you behave like the person you envision.

The things you do show what you are.
The things you fail to do speak loudly too.

First let Christ work in you.
Then you will live out your faith.

Being is basic to doing.
Being precedes working.

Being is God's business.
Being is the work of Christ in you.

> *Let us have no imitation Christian love.*
> *Let us have a genuine break with evil and*
> *a real devotion to good. Let us have warm*
> *affection for one another as between*
> *brothers, and a willingness to let the other*
> *man have the credit.*
> **—Romans 12:9, 10**

There is always plenty to *do* as a Christian.
But it is more important to *be* a Christian first.

Yet by doing we deepen the reality of being.
We learn by doing.

Only the loving know the meaning of love.
Only the beloved of God can truly love.

66

SNOBS?

"I don't like that man."
Charles Lamb was talking about a passing stranger.

"But Charles," replied his friend,
"you don't even know him."

"Of course I don't know him," said the essayist.
"If I knew him I couldn't dislike him."

We form our judgments quickly.
We make them on too little information.

If only we knew what others were like
we wouldn't be so snobbish and look down on them.

What makes us think we can get away with it,
that we can go right ahead being snobs?

Because it doesn't really matter?

Because we're Christians anyway?
Because we're secure in our faith?

Do we assign forgiveness to ourselves *before* we sin,
and then sin anyway, without any conscience?

Do we think God will never hold Christians
responsible?

What spells ruin for others
holds danger for us!

If *they* can't get away with it, neither can *we*,
even though we're Christians.

A person may even say,

"At least I'm being honest about it.
I'm a sinner. I admit it."

That isn't enough.

We ought not even to tolerate "small" sins.
They're never small in God's eyes.

When we persist in sin, we harden our hearts.
We stifle the voice of God.

This is idolatrous security.
This is hypocritical piety.
This is playing a game with the grace of God.

> *Live in harmony with each other. Don't
> become snobbish but take a real interest in
> ordinary people. . . . Don't say "It doesn't
> matter what people think," but see that
> your public behavior is above criticism.*
> **—Romans 12:16, 17**

Because of the grace of God,
I must not allow myself to willingly continue sinning.

I ought to learn to live in love.

67

HOW TO OVERCOME EVIL

A man in India became a Christian.

Shortly after his conversion he overheard
a few lawyers discussing Jesus.

One of them made a slanderous remark.

The young Christian took off his shoe
and struck the offender across the shoulders.

He left the men, feeling exceedingly righteous.
He had defended his Lord.

That night he thought about it again.
He prayed and then fell asleep.

He dreamed he saw Jesus coming toward him.
He expected to be congratulated.

Instead, as Jesus drew near,
He removed his robe and bared His shoulder.

There the Christian saw the marks of his shoes
on the shoulder of Jesus.

We can never overcome evil with evil.
We can only overcome evil with good.

We can never help others by our reaction.
We can only witness to them in love.

The blows we inflict on others
are blows inflicted on Christ.

What we do to the least of His brethren
we also do to Him.

Paul not only persecuted *Christians* before his
conversion.
He also persecuted *Christ*.

Christ identifies Himself with His people.

> *Never take vengeance into your own
> hands, my dear friends: stand back and let
> God punish if He will. . . . Don't allow
> yourself to be overpowered by evil. Take
> the offensive—overpower evil by good!*
> **—Romans 12:19, 21**

Suffer in silence.
Bear your trial willingly.

It will do far more than returning evil with evil.

How did *Jesus* return the evil which men did to Him?

68

CHRISTIAN CITIZENS

All over the world there are reactions
against the powers that be.

It seems fashionable to demonstrate.
Especially among the young.
College students are in rebellion.

Why is this so?

Mainly because the young are fed up with the old
line.
They are angry with man's bungling efforts for peace.

They cannot tolerate man's inhumanity.
They want to end wars.
They want to stop inequalities and hate.

They have a right to be angry.
The world is far from perfect.

Citizens should not be denied the privilege
of working for the betterment of man.

Governments are not to be dictatorships.

In a totalitarian state the people serve the
government.
In a democracy the government is to serve the
people.

"The democratic concept of man is false
because it is Christian. The democratic concept
holds that each man has a value as a sovereign being"
(Karl Marx).

Each man holds a value as an individual.

From this Christian emphasis comes our concept of government.

A Christian accepts his responsibility to the state.
He is to improve conditions.

He is to adhere to the law, pay taxes,
and behave like a decent citizen.

This even held true in the Roman world.

One Christian put it this way long ago:
"This is a very bad world, Donatus."

In spite of this fact Paul wrote,

> *Every Christian ought to obey the civil authorities, for all legitimate authority is derived from God's authority, and the existing authority is appointed under God. To oppose authority, then, is to oppose God.*
>
> **—Romans 13:1, 2**

One thing the young need to realize.
The old also desire justice and peace!

There may be corruption in government.
There will always be compromises.
There is also conscientious effort.

Some men mature through the experiences of life.
They are deeply affected by man's predicament.

A Christian should gain confidence in the powers that be.
A Christian sees them as established by God.

But this is never an invitation to complacency.
It is always a call to responsible living.

164

69

THE KEY OF LOVE

Three men had reservations in a certain hotel.
They discovered that their rooms were on the 31st
floor.

But the elevators were out of commission.
They had to climb the stairs.

To help the time pass,
they decided each should tell a story.

For the first ten floors one man would tell a funny
story.
For the next ten floors another man would tell a
heroic story.
For the last ten floors the third man would tell a sad
story.

By the time the three men reached the 24th floor,
the first two urged their friend to start in.

"Fellows," he began,
"I have the saddest story you ever heard."

Then he blurted out,
"I left the key in the lobby!"

I have a sadder story to tell.
The church has left the key behind.

The key of love.

Are we known for love of God and neighbor?
Are Christians characterized by love?

Or is the church known rather for its faith?
For its prayers rather than its kind actions?
For its worship rather than its good works?
For its doctrines rather than its deeds?

And sometimes for its legalism?
Legalism is not love.

Have we substituted our patterns of piety?

Are we more concerned about being a witness
than being a person?

About having our devotional life more than being
devoted?
Even about social action rather than Christian
behavior?

> *The man who loves his neighbor has
> obeyed the whole Law in regard to his
> neighbor. . . . Love hurts nobody;
> therefore love is the answer to the Law's
> commands.*
>
> **—Romans 13:8, 10**

The burning issue is not "how to be spiritual."
It is rather "the love of God and man."

> "The mind has a thousand eyes,
> The heart but one.
> Yet the light of a whole life dies
> When love is done."

Are we really convinced that love is
the essence of our faith?

70

WAKE UP TO REALITY

"Comedy of Errors" is a play about two brothers.

As the story unfolds, it is obvious that
these two brothers are estranged from each other.

They haven't seen each other for years.
But eventually they must meet.

Then comes the final scene.
The tension is tremendous.
Finally they will meet.

What if, instead of this happening on stage,
they meet somewhere else?

Then somebody comes running out from backstage:

"Boy, that was some meeting!
You should've seen what happened."

The audience would feel cheated.
It would be a terrible letdown.
Some might even demand their money back.

There must be a climax to our "play."
We will meet God.
But it won't happen backstage.

It will happen in the final act.

The curtain may soon come down on *this* act.
And then comes the climax of history.

Why all this stress on behavior? Because, as I think you have realized, the present time is of the highest importance—it is time to wake up to reality. Every day brings God's salvation nearer.

—Romans 13:11

This is why today is of the utmost importance. Today determines tomorrow.

We cannot live in the future. We must live in the present.

What we do now determines our destiny. There is no time to indulge ourselves.

Let us be Christ's men from head to foot, and give no chances to the flesh to have its fling.

—Romans 13:14

When the curtain falls, it will be too late.

Now is the time to live wide-awake lives.

71

CHRISTIAN BEHAVIOR

What every Christian wants to know is simply this:

What am I allowed to do as a Christian?
What are the rules and regulations of Christianity?

What is forbidden?
What is allowed?

Where are the boundaries?
Where are the fences?

Questions about murder, adultery, and stealing
we certainly know about.

We know we should not commit those "big" sins.
Nor should we be critical, unforgiving, or dishonest.

The Bible is clear about all this also.
But is a Christian allowed to drink, dance,
smoke, or go to the races?

Can he attend the movies?
What about looking at TV on Sundays?

"Do you think I'm wrong in not allowing my
fourteen-year-old daughter to wear a bikini?"
asked a mother disturbed about skimpy beachwear.

What does the Bible say about this?
Does it have any answers in black and white?

Here are two Christians who behave differently:
One is a vegetarian.
The other eats meat.

The vegetarian says a Christian ought not to eat
meat.

The other says it doesn't make any difference.

Are they both Christians?
Yes.

Should *one* rule be laid down for both?
Black or white?
Either/or?

The Bible lays down no rules in such matters!
It declares that God accepts them both.

What is even more important is this—
They should not criticize each other.

The vegetarian should not look down on the other:

"I'm a better Christian because I don't eat meat."

Nor should the meat-eater scorn the begetarian
because he isn't free to eat it.

> *The meat-eater should not despise the*
> *vegetarian, nor should the vegetarian con-*
> *demn the meat-eater—they should reflect*
> *that God has accepted them both. After*
> *all, who are you to criticize the servant of*
> *somebody else, especially when that*
> *Somebody Else is God?*
> **—Romans 14:3, 4**

If God has accepted both,
it's not worth bickering about.

As for your behavior,
you will have to be guided by Him.

God has given you His Spirit for that purpose.

72

ONE CODE FOR ALL CHRISTIANS?

When is a child too old to spank?

Doesn't that depend on the child?
You can't turn it off at fourteen for all.

Why must we have laws laid down for everything?
Why must everything be clearly stated?

Wouldn't that make it so much easier?
Of course it would.

If I knew exactly what was right or wrong,
I would merely consult the catalog.

I would then find smoking, drinking, or card-playing
listed as "sins" and would know what to avoid.

The Bible is not quite so simple.

When we are solely governed by rules,
we are actually in great danger.

We need no longer explore the mind of Christ.
Everything is indexed.

We know what is demanded of us.
We know what is not allowed.

And . . . *we stop growing!*

Our quest is finished.
We become fossilized Christians.

Christianity is not that pat.

It invites us into a living relationship with Christ.

Not into a static code.
Not into catalogued behavior.
Not into set ideas.

We are to search the Word of God and apply it.
And that is never easy.

> *Again, one man thinks some days of more importance than others. Another man considers them all alike. Let every one be definite in his own convictions.*
> **—Romans 14:5**

Everyone needs to be persuaded within.
If his conscience troubles him, he should not do it.

But someone else's conscience may not bother him.
That's his business.
Not yours.

Unless, of course, he is clearly going against
Scripture.

Otherwise, to lay down the same rules for everybody
fits all Christians into the same cans.

To look alike, act alike, be alike.
Labeled the same.

That's not good news!
Nor is it a dynamic relationship with God.

73

LIVING FOR GOD

"I am resolved never to do anything
which I should be afraid to do
if it were the last hour of my life" (Jonathan
Edwards).

That's a great way to live.
But it's not a life of fear.

The person who is afraid
cannot live in freedom.
He lives with restrictions upon him.

He serves the Lord,
not willingly, but running scared.

A free man lives as a child of God.

A child is not without responsibility.
A child is conscious of being a child.
A child wants to please his father.

The emotion of fear will leave you anyhow.
The reality of love will not.

Love is acting responsibly.
Love is a battle.
Love is maturing.

And love knows that we must give an account.

We will not have to answer to men.
We will have to answer to our Father.

We are accountable for our life.
And our deeds.

If we really think this through,
we will not worry too much about other people.

We have ourselves on our hands.
And that will be quite enough.

> *The truth is that we neither live nor die as self-contained units. At every turn life links us to God, and when we die we come face-to-face with Him.*
>
> **—Romans 14:8**

Therefore we need to keep asking ourselves,

"What kind of person am I?
What kind of person do I want to be?

Now that I have taken Christ into my life,
how should this affect me?

Do I really act as a Christian?
Or am I merely a Christian in word?

Am I guided by fear or by love?"

74

THE STRONG AND THE WEAK

There are both strong and weak Christians.

The strong should not despise the weak.
They may be able to do some things the weak cannot.
This should not give them a big head.

The weak should not judge the strong.
They may be able to do those things.
Not all Christians fit into the same can.
Nor do all follow the same code.

But the responsibility lies with the strong.
They should set a good example for the weak.

If they are really interested in people,
they will consider their "brothers" and "sisters."

Both the strong and the weak must receive
guidance from God.

A special evangelist conducts telephone evangelism.
He works in the city.
He calls people everywhere.

Sometimes he calls bars.
Sometimes his contacts lead him to these places.

Should he go there?
How else could he reach such people?

But what if a weak Christian saw him enter a bar?
What if some weak brother would be highly
offended?

Should the evangelist say,

"I can talk to you over the phone,

but I'm not allowed to enter your establishment?"

In saying that he puts himself above that person.
He is really saying,

"I'm better than you are because
I don't go to such places."

Therefore a rule cannot be laid down:
"Never must a Christian enter a bar."

A college girl said,

"The people in my church are only interested
to see whether I don't drink or smoke.
They're not interested in my real problems."

Christians cannot mold everyone into their own
image.

Husbands try to do that with their wives.
And wives with their husbands.

We ought to be molded into the image of Christ.
But that is *His* job.
Not ours.

> *Why, then, criticize your brother's actions,
> why try to make him look small? We shall
> all be judged one day, not by each other's
> standards or even our own, but by the
> standard of Christ.*
>
> **—Romans 14:10**

We'd better discover what *that* is all about.

It will certainly include an interest in persons.
And their real problems.

What really matters above all is pleasing Christ!

176

75

THE STANDARD

Al Ferrara, at one time with the Dodgers,
explained on a post-game show how he hit his home
run.

"I concentrate. I mean, I really concentrate,
and keep my mind a blank."

Now, it's not so easy to concentrate
and keep your mind a blank!

Particularly if you have your mind made up.

There are, of course, Christians whose minds are
already made up.

They tell you exactly what a Christian is supposed to
do.
And what he's not allowed to do.

This is generally the standard:

Don't smoke, drink, dance, or gamble.
Don't go to movies, races, or sports on Sundays.
Don't wear makeup and low-cut dresses.
Don't look at TV on Sundays or play cards.

There are many other rules.
All negative.

Those who keep them are good Christians.
All the others are inferior.
In a lower classification.

They haven't arrived among the select saints.

The dogmatists cannot find Scripture for all this.
They try hard to find it.

But—all the negatives in the world
don't add up to one positive.

Biblical Christianity is far more difficult.
There are no rules for questions of conscience.

Only following Christ.

The Communists make it easy:

"The government is my conscience.
Whatever the government demands we do."

Some church people have it easy:

"The church is my conscience.
Whatever the church allows we obey.
Whatever it condemns we shun."

The dogmatists have it easy too.
Their negatives are neatly established.

But a Christian has to confess,
"Christ is my conscience."

Christ Himself must guide our behavior.
Through Scripture.
By His Spirit.

But all questions are not settled.

*After all, the kingdom of heaven is not a
matter of whether you get what you like to*

eat and drink, but of righteousness and peace and joy in the Holy Spirit. . . . Put these things first in serving Christ.
          —Romans 14:17, 18

So, if your mind is already made up,
you can't actually concentrate on Christ.

Only an open mind can be receptive.

76

A SENSE OF CONVICTION

You have seen him.
He carries his Bible.

He wears a fixed smile.
He walks about with his nose up in the air.

He tries to be different.
He's very religious.

If you stop to talk to him,
he'll talk religion to you.

This is what bothers you.

If he wants to go to church, O.K.
If he wants to be religious, O.K.

But why can't he live a little?
Why can't he give a little?

Why does he have to take it with him everywhere?
Like *that*?

Whenever there's something fun to do,
a red light flashes on for him.
He stops.

There are always red lights flashing on for him.
All the time.
Everywhere.

When he's offered a cigarette, he says proudly,

"No thanks. *I* don't smoke.

The Lord took that from me.
I'm a Christian!"

That's not a testimony.
He's just slapped his friend across the face.

What he actually said was,
"You're not as pious as I am."

He may excuse himself from drinking
or smoking or such things.
But no one respects one who is "holier-than-thou."

The trouble with this religious crank is this:
He fears a nagging inner voice.

He was probably brought up by parents
who labeled everything taboo.

He was never allowed to think for himself.

He isn't free any longer.
He always reports in.

God does not desire parolees.
He wants liberated men and women.

> *Your personal convictions are a matter of*
> *faith between yourself and God. . . . When*
> *we act apart from our faith we sin.*
> **—Romans 14:22, 23**

Taking things out of your life
hardly makes you a Christian.

It just makes you empty.

You must put something in too!

77

LIFE TOGETHER

We want people to like us for ourselves!

If you say,
"I don't care about that;
it really doesn't matter whether people like me,"
You're probably not telling the truth.

The more some protest,
the more they really want it.

They may often have been hurt.
Even so, they still desire to be liked.

But what if someone asks you questions
and makes a pleasant approach
only after having buttered you up
to ask for your vote in an election?

Or tries to sell you something?
Or maybe invites you to his church?

You don't go for that.
You want people to like you for *yourself*.

You are tired of fault-finders.
You don't enjoy critics.

Why do people always overlook the good?

Even a cow eating a bundle of hay with a briar in it
will munch the hay and leave the briar.

Why can't people be like that?

Our desires are normal—
To be liked, appreciated, affirmed.

If *you* feel that way about it,
don't you think other people do too?

Don't others want to be accepted,
just as you desire acceptance?

Your friendship should be warm and real.
Everybody else needs it as much as you do.

> *So open your hearts to one another as Christ has opened His heart to you, and God will be glorified.*
> **—Romans 15:7**

How has Christ opened His heart to you?

In love.
In grace.
In freedom.
In truth.

He accepts you as you are.
Can you accept others as they are?

Our life together would undergo a revolution
if we really believed this.

And *practiced* it.

78

A RADIANT LIFE

The Devil never invented a single pleasure.
God did.

All the Devil's enticements are perversions.

Healthy eating and drinking results
in simple and wholesome living.

Gluttony never brings happiness.
It creates overweight problems and puts you on a
diet.

Intemperate drinking brings alcoholism.
Problems for the individual and society.

Money is a great servant
but a terrible master.

When we seek first God's kingdom,
all things will be added unto us.

When we seek first all things,
we are in bondage to materialism.

Sex was created by God.

But perversion and misuse bring about boredom,
frustration, guilt, even impotence.

God wants man to enjoy life.
The Devil ruins it for us.

Christ left us a legacy of peace and joy.

But the Devil makes tawdy substitutes.

> *May the God of hope fill you with joy and peace in your faith, that by the power of the Holy Spirit your whole life and outlook may be radiant with hope.*
> **—Romans 15:13**

Everyone desires happiness.
Everyone wants to enjoy life.

Here's how.

It is the gift of God.
Through His Spirit.

You receive it by faith.

Faith can be most effective.

Like catching a cold.
Only through faith you catch a *good* infection.

Happiness and peace are the results of faith.
That's what happens when you put yourself in God's hands.

It leads to a radiant life.
And true pleasure.

79

A WATCHFUL EYE

There will always be wolves in sheep's clothing.
Weeds among the wheat.
Bad trees among the good.
Good and bad fish caught in the same net.

The false will invade the true.
The counterfeit will appear among the real.

Evil in many forms continues to seduce man.
We are never entirely free from it.

The last battle has not yet been fought.
Evil remains man's predicament.
Only God can deliver him from it.

These wolves look like sheep.
They sound like sheep.
They talk like sheep.

The weeds resemble the wheat.
The bad trees make early promises.

> *Keep a watchful eye on those who cause*
> *trouble and make difficulties among you,*
> *in plain opposition to the teaching you*
> *have been given, and steer clear of them.*
> *Such men do not really serve our Lord*
> *Jesus Christ at all but are utterly self-*
> *centered. Yet with their plausible and*
> *attractive arguments they deceive those*

who are too simple-hearted to see through them.

—Romans 16:17, 18

The simplicity of faith will overcome
the complexity of the false.

God's grace will overshadow all arguments.

Keep yourselves in God.
And God will keep you.

But also keep a watchful eye.

80

500 YEARS FROM NOW

Johnny Carson asked a question of his guest:

"Would you rather go back into history
or forward into the future?"

His guest said she'd rather go back into history.

Then Carson added:
"I'd like to go ahead 500 years
and see where we've been."

We're going to be around 500 years from now.
5,000 years from now.
5,000,000 years from now.

If there is a God.
If there is eternity.

Christ has ascended the throne.
The time is drawing near.

The defeat of Satan is imminent:

> **It will not be long before the God of peace
> will crush Satan under your feet.**
> **—Romans 16:20**

The time to think about all this is *now*.
This is the beginning of the end.

We are destined for eternity.
We are to live as if it were here already.

The final victory is not merely in the future.

The final victory must influence the present.

James Calvert set out as a missionary to Fiji. Everyone tried to stop him.

En route aboard ship even the captain warned him about the cannibals on the islands.

"You will risk your life among such savages!"

James Calvert made a magnificent reply: "We died before we came here."

That's the way to prepare for 500 years from now. And all the rest of eternity.

> *May the grace of our Lord Jesus Christ be with you.*
>
> **—Romans 16:20**

Now.

A FINAL WORD

You have just become familiar with the central ideas of Paul's Letter to Rome. You have entered into the thought of Paul and his teaching of the Christian faith.

It has not been an exhaustive study, nor was it meant to be. Two roads remain before you:

(1) You may wish to read Romans in its entirety. You are now better prepared to understand it. You ought to read it in a modern-speech translation.

(2) You may wish to do a more exhaustive study of the Letter. Then consult a commentary. Take notes as you read, think for yourself, and apply daily what you learn.

Martin Luther called Romans "a bright light, almost enough to illumine all the Scripture." In his introduction to the Epistle he writes: "Every Christian should . . . occupy himself with it every day, as the daily bread of the soul. It can never be read or pondered too much, and the more it is dealt with the more precious it becomes, and the better it tastes."

✿　✿　✿

Now—how about you? Have you responded to the invitation to enter the family of God?

Day Brighteners from Romans

Here is a summary, from Romans, on how this can happen:

° Admit your sin (Romans 3:19, 23).

   ° Accept the Savior (Romans 3:24, 28).

      ° Affirm your faith (Romans 5:1, 2).

         ° Assert your freedom (Romans 8:1, 14, 15).

           ° Acknowledge your commitment (Romans 12:1, 2).

           ° Attain your destiny (Romans 14:8, 9).

Now to Him who is able to set you on your feet as His own sons—according to my gospel, according to the preaching of Jesus Christ Himself . . . to Him, I say, the only God who is wise, be glory forever through Jesus Christ.

—Romans 16:25, 27